符号中国 SIGNS OF CHINA

笔墨纸砚

WRITING BRUSH, INK STICK, PAPER AND INKSTONE

"符号中国"编写组 ◎ 编著

中央民族大学出版社
China Minzu University Press

图书在版编目(CIP)数据

笔墨纸砚：汉文、英文 / "符号中国"编写组编著. — 北京：中央民族大学出版社, 2024.9
（符号中国）
ISBN 978-7-5660-2296-7

Ⅰ.①笔…　Ⅱ.①符…　Ⅲ.①文化用品—介绍—中国—汉、英　Ⅳ.①K875.4

中国国家版本馆CIP数据核字（2024）第016791号

符号中国：笔墨纸砚　WRITING BRUSH, INK STICK, PAPER AND INKSTONE

编　　著	"符号中国"编写组
策划编辑	沙　平
责任编辑	满福玺
英文编辑	邱　械
美术编辑	曹　娜　郑亚超　洪　涛
出版发行	中央民族大学出版社
	北京市海淀区中关村南大街27号　邮编：100081
	电话：（010）68472815（发行部）　传真：（010）68933757（发行部）
	（010）68932218（总编室）　　　　（010）68932447（办公室）
经 销 者	全国各地新华书店
印 刷 厂	北京兴星伟业印刷有限公司
开　　本	787 mm×1092 mm　1/16　印张：11.75
字　　数	162千字
版　　次	2024年9月第1版　2024年9月第1次印刷
书　　号	ISBN 978-7-5660-2296-7
定　　价	58.00元

版权所有　侵权必究

"符号中国"丛书编委会

唐兰东　巴哈提　杨国华　孟靖朝　赵秀琴

本册编写者

季孙歈

前言 Preface

　　笔、墨、纸、砚是中国古代文房用具中的代表，被历代中国文人视为至宝。它们不仅是中国古代书画艺术的载体和组成部分，也体现着中国古代文人的生活情趣。

　　在中国5000年的历史长河中，中国人不断开拓创新，形成了自己独特的文化传承体系。作为中国传统文化的代表性符号之一的笔、墨、纸、砚，凝聚着传统文化的精髓，它们不仅演绎出中国古代书画艺术的神韵，记录下了中华民族的辉煌历史，其本身也闪耀着独特的

　　Traditionally, ink stick, inkstone, paper and writing brush were four treasures of Chinese scholars. These four were indispensable in writing, painting and calligraphy, and also something to show a refined taste.

　　Over the past five thousand years, by continuous efforts to innovate and invent, Chinese people created a brilliant culture. Ink stick, inkstone, paper and writing brush, as the symbols of this culture, became four unique blooms in the garden of Chinese civilization. Thanks to these inventions, Chinese calligraphic and painting art flourished and Chinese history was recorded. These four were no longer only tools, they became works of art. Even today, they still play an important role in Chinese painting and calligraphy.

　　With text in Chinese and English

艺术光芒。今天，笔、墨、纸、砚仍然在中国传统书画创作中发挥着重要的作用，是现代文具中一道亮丽的风景线。

本书以中英文对照的形式，配以大量精美图片，向海内外读者分别展示了笔、墨、纸、砚的发展历程、品种及收藏名品，希望能够带领读者了解中国书房文化、体会不同文房用具的艺术魅力。

and illustrations and photos, we attempt to probe into their origins and styles, and record their developments and symbolic collections in this book. With this book, we hope to help you get to know the inner world of Chinese literati and appreciate the allure of literati traditions.

目 录 Contents

笔墨纸砚——中国人的文房四宝
Writing Brush, Ink Stick, Paper and Inkstone——
Collectively Called "Four Treasures of a Chinese Study" 001

笔
The Writing Brush.. 003

笔的历史
History of Writing Brush...................................... 004

毛笔的种类
Varieties of Writing Brushes.................................. 031

笔中名品
Famous Varieties.. 041

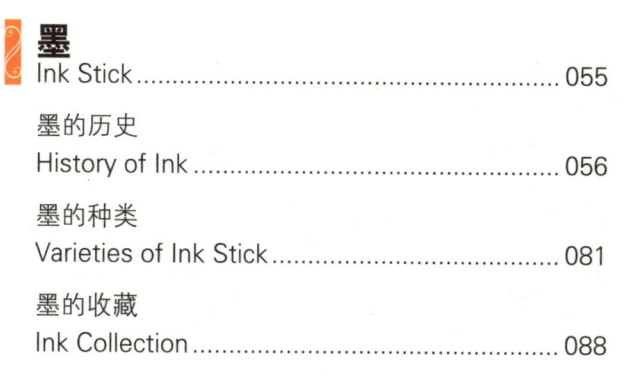

墨
Ink Stick... 055

墨的历史
History of Ink.. 056

墨的种类
Varieties of Ink Stick.. 081

墨的收藏
Ink Collection.. 088

纸
Paper 093

纸的历史
History of Paper 094

纸的种类
Varieties of Paper 120

砚
Inkstone 129

砚的历史
History of Inkstone 130

古砚的种类
Varieties of Antique Inkstone 145

四大名砚
The Most Famous Four Varieties 151

附录：其他文房用具
Appendix: Other Tools in a Traditional Chinese Study 161

笔墨纸砚——中国人的文房四宝
Writing Brush, Ink Stick, Paper and Inkstone——Collectively Called "Four Treasures of a Chinese Study"

笔、墨、纸、砚合称"文房四宝",是四种中国古代的文房用具。"文房"原指官府掌管文书的部门,后来专指文人的书房。最先把笔、墨、纸、砚称为"文房四宝"的是北宋的苏易简,他在其所作《文房四谱》中对笔、墨、纸、砚进行了详细的论述,"文房四宝"由此得名。

These four treasures refer to ink sticks, inkstones, paper and writing brushes a scholar in the old days kept in his study. "Study" in Chinese is "*Wenfang*", which originally means governmental departments in charge of record making and keeping. Later, this word means exclusively the study. The first one in history who ever used the phrase "the four treasures of the study" was Su Yijian of the Northern Song Dynasty. In his writing *Wenfang Sipu* or *The Four Treasures of the Study*, he detailed each of them. Thus the phrase was born.

文房四宝中，除纸出现稍晚外，笔、墨、砚都有着悠久的历史。在漫长的发展过程中，文房四宝的制作水平与日俱增，涌现了不少名工巧匠。他们精选名材，施展精湛的技艺，创造了大量的文房精品，为中国传统文化留下了灿烂的遗产。

笔、墨、纸、砚是中国古代文人必备的文房用具，因此其几千年的发展都是在古代文人的关注与参与下进行的。从器形到纹饰，从选材到制作，都凝结着古代文人的文化素养和审美观念。

Apart from paper that came later, the rest three have a long history. During which time craftsmanship was perfected and master makers appeared to leave legendary works behind with the best materials they could get and matchless skills they had honed. Their works are treasures of traditional culture.

The four were indispensable to study and their progress involved active efforts from scholars. From their shape and decorative pattern to the material chosen and making techniques, everything showed a scholarly taste in ancient times.

- 传统文房（现代）
书桌上摆放着各式传统文房用具，与墙上悬挂的书法、古朴的家具相得益彰。
Study in Traditional Style (Modern Times)
On the desk are traditional things needed in the study, which match perfectly with calligraphic works hanging on the wall and traditional-style furniture around.

笔
The Writing Brush

　　文房四宝中的"笔"是指"毛笔"。毛笔是中国古代先民所创造的书画工具，由兽毛捆缚于笔管制成。笔头柔软富有弹性，能够表现出汉字点、撇、横、捺的变化及中国山水画的浓淡起伏。毛笔位居文房四宝之首，其使用和普及是中国文化兴盛的标志。

One of the four treasures, the writing brush, an invention by distant ancestors, is made by binding animal hairs to the end of the brush holder. The hairs are soft and resilient, able to write different strokes of a Chinese character and paint dark or pale strokes of Chinese landscape painting. Always as the first one mentioned of the four, the writing brush with its popularity and extensive usage marked the progress of Chinese culture.

> ## 笔的历史

中国人使用毛笔的历史十分悠久，最原始的毛笔出现在距今10000—4000年的新石器时代，此后经过不断改良，至魏晋时期方基本定型。唐代（618—907）之后，宣笔、湖笔的出现是制笔工艺迅速发展的标志。明清时期，毛笔已成为文房中必不可少的工具，其造型、纹饰及工艺更加精湛。

毛笔的起源

关于毛笔起源于何时，至今尚无定论。历史上有"蒙恬造笔"的传说。蒙恬是秦朝名将，有"中华第一勇士"之誉，然而这位勇士却与毛笔的起源有着密切的联系。

相传蒙恬带兵在外作战，要定期写战报呈送秦王，由于没有便利

> ## History of Writing Brush

China has a long history of using writing brushes. The earliest ones appeared about sometime between ten thousand and four thousand years ago during the Neolithic Age. Later, they experienced repeated innovations until the Wei and Jin dynasties when their design was finalized. After the Tang Dynasty (618-907), the appearance of the famous *Xuan* and *Hu* styles signified the fast development of the technique of making brushes. By the Ming and Qing dynasties, writing brushes had become indispensable in anyone's study and their design, decorative pattern and craftsmanship reached a level never obtained before.

Origin of Writing Brush

It is still an open question as for the time when the writing brush was invented,

• **蒙恬塑像**

蒙恬（？—前210），秦朝著名将领，因对毛笔的改良做出重大贡献而被人们尊奉为"笔祖"。

Statue of Meng Tian

Meng Tian (?-210 B.C.), a famous army general of the Qin Dynasty, was taken as the ancestor of the writing brush because of a significant innovation he made on this writing tool.

的书写工具，战报常常延期送到，为此蒙恬多次受罚。一天，蒙恬看见一只被箭射伤的兔子，它的尾巴在地上拖出了血迹，便有了灵感。他剪下一些兔尾毛，插在竹管上，试着用它来写字。他将兔毛做的笔往墨盘里一蘸，发现写字竟然非常流畅。后来蒙恬将这种制笔工艺推

yet a legend ascribed it to Meng Tian, an army general of the Qin Dynasty (221 B.C.-206 B.C.) with unusual military exploits to his name. He was regarded as "number one warrior of the nation". Obviously, he had something to do with the invention of the writing brush.

Each time he was out on battlefields, as the legend says, he was supposed to send reports about war progress to the Qin ruler at regular intervals. Yet, due to the lack of convenient writing tools, his reports were often past due. Meng Tian was often reprimanded and even penalized because of this. One day, after viewing a wounded rabbit leaving a trail of blood on the ground, he got an idea. He cut some hairs from the dead rabbit, which he tied to the end of a brush holder, with which he tried to pick up ink. Much to his excitement, it worked wonderfully. So he promoted this invention. This is why later generations take him as the inventor.

It's a legend after all. In fact, the writing brush appeared much earlier than in the Qin Dynasty (221 B.C.-206 B.C.). Unearthed objects prove that people in the Neolithic Age already used something like a brush to write. The decorative patterns appearing on the painted pottery

广开来，人们因此将蒙恬视为制笔的始祖。

　　传说终归是传说，事实上，毛笔的出现远早于秦朝（前221—前206）。从出土文物提供的证据来看，最迟在新石器时代就有类似毛笔的工具产生了。在新石器时代遗址出土的一些彩陶上，有刻意描绘的纹饰图案。这些纹饰清晰流畅，显然不是质地坚硬的刻画工具所能完成的，而应是由柔软的类似毛笔的工具描绘而成。因此考古学家推断新石器时代就已经出现了毛笔的雏形。

unearthed in relic sites from this period have flowing lines elaborately drawn, obviously not by a hard-tip writing tool but something with a very soft tip, something just like writing brush. According to archeologists, the Neolithic Age was the time when the earliest form of the writing brush appeared.

- 供奉笔祖蒙恬尊像碑记
  Stone Inscription on the Stele for Meng Tian, Inventor of Writing Brushes

新石器时代彩陶

新石器时代随着制陶工艺的成熟,在陶器器表或内壁进行彩绘的装饰手法逐渐流行起来。比较具有代表性的有黄河上游的马家窑文化(距今5000—4000年)、黄河中游的仰韶文化(距今7000—5000年)及黄河下游的大汶口文化(距今6000—4000年)等遗址中出土的一大批彩陶制品。这些陶器表面的纹饰大多以类似毛笔的工具绘制而成,黑色为主要基调,以几何纹饰为主,其他纹饰也大多以简单的线条为元素构成。

Painted Pottery During the Neolithic Age

With the maturity of pottery making in the Neolithic Age, decoration applied to outside and inside walls became popular. In this, representative works were found in Majiayao Culture (5000-4000 years ago) on the upper ranges of the Yellow River, the Yangshao Culture (7000-5000 years ago) on the middle ranges of the Yellow River and the Dawenkou Culture (6000-4000 years ago) on the lower ranges of the Yellow River. Many have black geometric shapes drawn by some brush-like tools. Some have simple lines only.

- 网格纹彩陶船形壶(仰韶文化)
Pottery Boat-shape Pot with Painted Grids(Yangshao Culture, 7000-5000 years ago)

- 豆荚纹彩陶钵(仰韶文化)
Painted Pottery Bowl with Bean Pattern(Yangshao Culture, 7000-5000 years ago)

- 鸟纹彩陶壶(马家窑文化)
Pottery Pot with a Bird Pattern (Majiayao Culture, 5000-4000 years ago)

- 花叶纹小口彩陶壶(大汶口文化)
Small-mouth Pottery Pot Painted with Flower Patterns (Dawenkou Culture, 6000-4000 years ago)

在河南安阳殷墟出土的甲骨片上也残留有朱书与墨迹，应为毛笔所书。所以，毛笔的起源是在殷商（前1600—前1046）之前，而不是秦朝蒙恬所创。1954年，在湖南省长沙市左家公山战国楚墓出土了一支毛笔，这是目前发现的最早的毛笔。1958年，在河南省信阳市长关台战国楚墓中也出土了一支竹杆毛笔，在制作结构和使用方法上都与左家公山战国楚墓出土的毛笔相似。

Characters in cinnabar and ink were also found in oracle bones unearthed in the Yin Dynasty ruins of Anyang, Henan Province, and were supposed to have been done by a writing brush. The Yin Dynasty, also called Shang (1600 B.C.-1046 B.C.), was much earlier than Meng Tian's time and this proved beyond doubt the invention of the writing brush was not accredited to Meng Tian. In 1954, a writing brush in its true form was discovered in Zuojiagong Mount of Changsha, Hunan Province, from a Chu tomb of the Warring States Period (475 B.C.-221 B.C.). That was the earliest writing brush ever found. In 1958, another writing brush with a bamboo holder was found in Changguantai, Xinyang of Henan Province, also from a Chu tomb. The two were very similar in form and craftsmanship.

- **毛笔（战国）**
  这支毛笔是中国迄今发现最早的毛笔，被称为"战国笔"，又因其出土于楚墓而称为"楚笔"。笔头是用兔毛制成，笔杆是竹制的，笔头用丝缠绕绑扎成束包扎在笔杆的外侧，再封漆固定。
  Writing Brush (Warring States Period, 475 B.C.-221 B.C.)
  This writing brush, the oldest ever found in China, is called "the writing brush from the Warring States Period" or "the Chu writing brush" from the tomb in which it was found. It had rabbit hairs and a bamboo holder. The hairs were fastened to one end before the lacquer was applied to make it stronger.

"笔"字的演变
Changes in history on the character "writing brush"

𦘒 → 筆 → 筆 → 笔

金文→篆书→繁体字→简体字
Bronze Inscription—Seal Script—Traditional Character—Simplified Form

- 金文里（聿）字像（手）持（聿），篆书中则是在"聿"字上加了"竹"构成"笔"字。

  The bronze inscription, a style from the inscriptions often found on ancient bronze objects, is a pictograph resembling a hand holding something, while the seal script has the word "bamboo" in it to complete the meaning of "writing brush".

秦汉时期的毛笔

秦代（前221—前206）以前，毛笔多以枯木为笔杆。秦始皇统一六国后，在文化方面统一了文字，实行"书同文"，规定"篆书"为统一字体，毛笔的使用也由此推广至全国。此时，毛笔形成了竹管、兽毫合成的基本形制，有些地方已经开始因制作毛笔而著称。另外，秦代已经出现用细竹管制成的中部镂空的笔管套。

汉代（前206—公元220）时，

Writing Brushes Made During the Qin and Han Dynasties

Before the Qin Dynasty (221B.C.-206 B.C.), most writing brushes had holders from weathered wood. After Qin Shihuang, the first emperor of the Qin Dynasty who unified China and promoted a unified written language that took the seal script as the only style permissible to use, using writing brush became a nationwide practice. By then, the structure of the writing brush had taken shape, a bamboo holder with a tip

毛笔的制造工艺得到了进一步的发展。笔头除了用兔毛、羊毛外，还出现了将狼毛、鹿毛、狸毛混合制成的"兼毫笔"。兼毫笔的笔头多以兔毫为笔柱，羊毛裹在兔毫的外面，使毛笔的特性因混合比例不同而形成差异，满足了不同书写者的需要。笔管的质地和装饰在汉代也逐渐引起人们的注意，据文献记载，当时的笔管已有"雕以黄金，饰以和璧，缀以隋珠，文以翡翠"的情况，十分华丽。

汉代还有一种"簪白笔"，是一种笔管长约20厘米，笔尾部削成尖形，并髹之以漆的毛笔。

of animal hairs. Some places made fame out of their making. About this time, the writing brush cap appeared in the form of a hollow bamboo tube.

Further progress was made during the Han Dynasty (206 B.C.-220 A.D.). Apart from rabbit or goat hairs, hairs from other animals like weasel, deer and leopard cats were used together, called *Jianhao*, for better performance. Usually, *Jianhao* had rabbit hairs in the middle and goat hairs around, mixed with different percentages to satisfy different needs. Penholders' material and decoration began to draw attention. In history records, some writing brushes made then had gold, jade, pearl and emerald as decoration.

A new variety appeared in the Han Dynasty, *Zanbai* (literally, hairpin white) writing brush, 20 centimeters long on the holder pointed at one end and coated with lacquer.

- 狼毫笔（汉）
Writing Brush with Weasel Hairs
(Han Dynasty, 206B.C.-220A.D.)

- 竹杆羊毫笔（秦）

1975年在湖北省云梦睡虎地秦墓中出土了三支以竹为管的毛笔，这是其中一支。竹管的前端被凿出孔，笔头嵌入其中。

Writing Brush Made with Bamboo and Goat Hairs (Qin Dynasty, 221B.C.-206B.C.)

Three writing brushes with bamboo holders were discovered in a Qin-dynasty tomb in 1975 in Hubei Province. This is one of the three, whose end is hollowed to receive brush hairs.

簪白笔

汉代文官奏事，常用毛笔将所奏之事写在笏（古代官员上朝时拿着的手板，多由竹片制成）上，写完之后即将毛笔插在发髻或帽子上。后来这种做法逐渐演变成一种官服制度，凡文官上朝，皆须插笔，笔尖不蘸墨汁，纯粹用作装饰，称"簪白笔"。

Zanbai Writing Brush

Civil officials during the Han Dynasty appeared before the throne with a memo written on a bamboo slip they held in hand and a writing brush either in their hair or headwear. This practice progressed into a fashion. Every civil official appeared in court wore a writing brush, with no ink on its tip as a hairpin just for decoration purpose.

簪
Zan (hairpin)

笏
Hu (bamboo hand board)

- 汉代文官像
Civil Official of the Han Dynasty

魏晋南北朝时期的毛笔

魏晋南北朝时期，毛笔的发展不仅没有受到社会动荡的影响，而且形成了新的特点。这一时期，人们习惯跪坐在矮儿前悬肘书写，为了便于书写，笔杆的部分逐渐变短，笔锋的弹性得到加强，以"鼠须笔""紫毫笔"为代表的短杆笔深受文人的喜爱。中国书法史上的名作《兰亭序》便是"书圣"王羲之用"鼠须笔"（松鼠的尾毫所制）所作。

Writing Brushes Made During the Wei, Jin, Southern and Northern Dynasties

During the period of these dynasties, writing brush making continued to progress in spite of social turbulences. People on their knees wrote on a low desk with their wrists never touching it. For convenience writing brushes made in this time became shorter on the holder but more elastic on the tip. Popular styles were squirrel tail hairs and dark hairs from hares, very much favored by scholars. With a brush of the former style calligraphy sage Wang Xizhi did his immortal work in Chinese history, *Lanting Xu* or *The Preface to the Collection of Writings in Lanting*.

- 矮几（现代）
矮几的四足较短，书写时需跪坐在前。
Low Desk (Modern Times)
Because of its short legs, one had to write while kneeling beside a desk like this.

王羲之与《兰亭序》

王羲之（303—361，一作321—379），字逸少，祖籍琅琊临沂（今属山东省），后迁会稽（今浙江省绍兴市），中国东晋书法家，有"书圣"之称。他出身名门望族，其家族曾助东晋建朝于建康（今江苏省南京市）。王羲之曾官至右军将军，会稽内史，人称"王右军""王会稽"。世人对王羲之印象最深的是他的书法，他善隶、草、楷、行等各种字体的书法，而他的名作《兰亭序》被誉为"天下第一行书"，为历代书法家所推崇。

• 王羲之像
Wang Xizhi

Wang Xizhi and his *Lan Ting Xu*

Wang Xizhi (303-361 or 321-379), a calligraphy in the Eastern Jin Dynasty, courtesy name Yishao, came from Linyi in present-day Shandong Province but later moved to Kuaiji, today's Shaoxing in Zhejiang Province. Because he once served in the army as a general, he was also called with respect "Right General Wang" or "Wang Kuaiji". As a great master in all styles of writing his calligraphy was legendary. *Lanting Xu* was an immortal work in running script admired throughout history.

• 《兰亭序》【局部】王羲之（晋）

《兰亭序》作于东晋穆帝永和九年（353年）。当时王羲之与谢安、孙绰等41人，会于山阴（今浙江绍兴）兰亭，众人作了几十首诗汇集起来，公推德高望重的王羲之写一序文，记录这次雅集。王羲之在酒兴之下，用鼠须笔写下了28行324字，被后人誉为"天下第一行书"的《兰亭序》。

Lanting Xu (Partial), by Wang Xizhi (Jin Dynasty, 265-420)

This calligraphic work was done in 353, the ninth year of the Yonghe Period of Emperor Mu of the Eastern Jin Dynasty on a drinking party with 41 friends in Shanyin (present-day Shaoxing, Zhejiang Province). They composed poems over wine. Wang Xizhi was asked to write a foreword for the collection of these poems, which he did in a tipsy condition with a writing brush of squirrel tail hairs. This was how this immortal work, described as the best calligraphic piece in running script ever made, totaling 324 characters in 28 lines, was born.

笔 The Writing Brush

魏晋南北朝时期，毛笔的制作受到当时奢侈之风的影响，笔管的材质出现了金银、象牙、犀角、玉石等名贵材料，有的笔管上还雕刻有精美的图案作为装饰。《太平广记》中就记载有梁元帝曾有金、银、竹三管笔，分别用于记录不同品行、地位之人的事迹：忠孝两全者以金管笔书写；德行高尚者以银管笔书写；文章华丽者以斑竹笔书写。

Due to a craze for luxury among the rich and powerful during the Wei, Jin, Southern and Northern dynasties, materials for penholders also took a turn for expensive materials like gold, silver, ivory, rhinoceros horn or jade, some having elaborate decoration to go with. By *Taiping Guangji* or *The Encyclopedia of the Taiping Period,* Emperor Yuan of the Liang Dynasty had three writing brushes, gold, silver and bamboo, to record the conducts of his ministers: the gold for those loyal to him and pious to their parents, the silver for those of virtues and the bamboo for writers in a flowery style.

- 梁元帝的金、银、竹笔（南朝）

从左到右依次为银笔、金笔、竹笔。

The Gold, Silver and Bamboo Writing Brushes Emperor Yuan of Liang Used (the Southern Dynasties, 420-589)

From left to right they are silver, gold and the bamboo writing brushes.

江淹梦笔

江淹，南朝文学家。传说他小时候曾经梦见一位老先生送给他一支五色笔，此后，他的诗文就非常出色。后来，他又梦见五色笔被那位先生索回，原本才思敏捷的江淹则文思枯竭，人们评价他为"江郎才尽"。

"江淹梦笔"的典故中将毛笔作为评断勤学苦练的指标，也是才思的代表。典故中的江淹因为梦到毛笔而文思泉涌，因为梦见失笔而才尽，可见毛笔在文人心目中的价值。

Jiang Yan Receiving Brush In Dream

Jiang Yan, a man of letters during the Southern dynasties, once had a dream in which he received a five-color writing brush from someone. With the brush, as the legend says, he was able to write excellent articles to surprise everyone. Later, also in his dream, the brush was taken back by the man who had given it to him and from this time on his literary talent was no more. So came the popular saying "The imaginative power for writing is gone" for someone whose inspiration had dried up.

In this story, the writing brush was personified as the logo of hard work and talent. With it, Jiang Yan was able to write marvelous writings and without it, he had no inspiration left. It can be seen the value of the writing brush in the minds of the literati.

• 杭州"邵芝岩"笔庄的湖笔
Hu Style Brushes, from Shaozhiyan in Hangzhou

隋唐时期的毛笔

隋唐时期是毛笔发展的一个重要时期，出现了第一个制笔中心——宣州（今安徽省宣城市），著名的"宣笔"即产于此地。宣笔在选材、制作、性能上都超过了前代，其笔头坚挺，满足了当时人们席地而坐的书写需求。宣笔在隋唐时期风行一时，唐代朝廷用笔多为宣州所制。

Writing Brushes Made During the Sui and Tang Dynasties

These two dynasties saw fast progress in writing brush making. Xuanzhou (present-day Xuancheng of Anhui Province) appeared as the first center for brush making business China ever had in history. The writing brush made in this place was called "*Xuan*-style Writing Brush" for its better material, better making technology and function than those in previous dynasties. The hairs became harder, satisfied the needs of writing when sitting on the floor. Instantly, the use of *Xuan* style writing brush became a vogue during the Sui and Tang dynasties. Inside the Tang court, *Xuan* brushes were widely used.

宣笔

宣笔是中国古代著名的书画笔。宣州自秦代时已有制笔业，宣笔见于正史始于汉代。东晋时期（317—420），宣州陈氏是著名的制笔世家，其用山兔毛制成的一种紫毫毛笔，笔锋坚挺耐用，易于书写，但产量不高故很难买到。大书法家王羲之都曾向陈氏求笔。唐代（618—907）时，宣州成为全国的制笔中心。当时大江南北都有专门的制笔作坊，出现了诸葛氏、吕道人、汪伯立等制笔名家，宣笔发展到天下独尊的地位，一直到元代时才被后起的湖笔所取代。

The *Xuan* Style Writing Brushes

The *Xuan* style writing brush was famous for writing and painting in ancient China. Back in the Qin Dynasty writing brush making appeared in Xuanzhou. The earliest official documentation of brush making happened in the Han Dynasty. Later, during the Eastern Jin Dynasty, Xuanzhou had its famous family business in this trade, the Chen Family. The brushes made with dark hairs from mountain rabbits were unable to meet the huge market need. Even the calligraphy sage Wang Xizhi longed for one. Later, during the Tang Dynasty, Xuanzhou became the center of this trade in the country. Family businesses mushroomed along the Yangtze with big names like Zhuge, Lv Daoren and Wang Boli. *Xuan* style writing brushes dominated the market until the Yuan Dynasty when writing brushes from Huzhou rose to take away the glory.

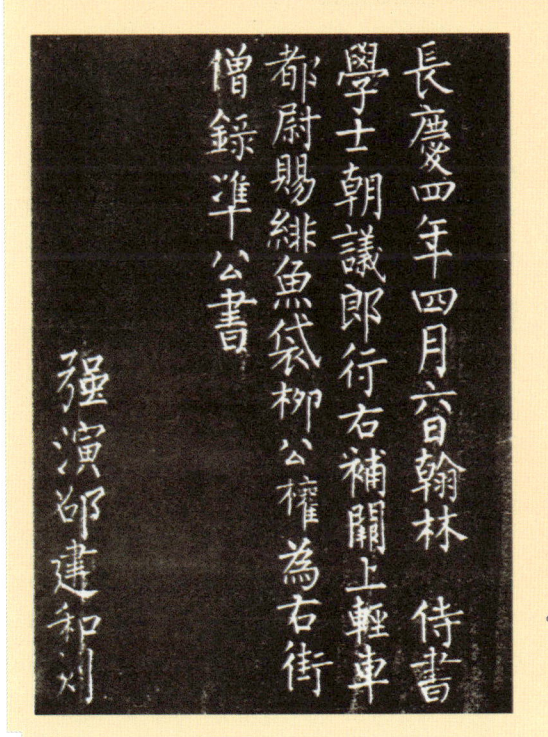

- 柳公权像

柳公权（778—865），字诚悬，唐代著名书法家。他善写楷书，与当时另一位书法家颜真卿齐名。

Liu Gongquan

Liu Gongquan (778-865), style name Chengxuan, famous calligrapher in the Tang Dynasty. His strong hand was the regular script and he enjoyed the same prestige as another calligraphy artist, his contemporary Yan Zhenqing.

- 《金刚经》【局部】柳公权（唐）

Vajracchedika-sutra [Partial], by Liu Gongquan (Tang Dynasty, 618-907)

- **宣笔（现代）**

Xuan Style Writing Brushes (Modern Times)

宣笔以选料严格、精工细作著称，具有毛纯耐用、刚柔适中、尖圆齐健"四德"兼全的独特风格。

Xuan style brushes are famous for their strict material selection and painstaking craft in making. The hairs they use are endurable, soft and vigorous, able to meet all the requirements for a nice brush.

隋唐时期制笔沿用魏晋时期的方法，制造锋短、形如鸡距的"鸡距笔"。后来因其吸墨性不好且易干枯，制笔工匠又改进制造出锋长柔软、吸墨性好的长锋笔。长锋笔书写流畅，适合行草书写，它的出现成就了以张旭、怀素为代表的草书大家，为唐宋书法带来了纵横洒脱的新风。

Writing brushes made during the Sui and Tang dynasties followed the way of the previous Wei and Jin dynasties, having short brush tips. Later, this short tip style was abandoned simply because it picked up little ink and dried up easily. They were replaced by soft long-hair brush tips much better in absorbing ink for continuous writing, perfect for running and cursive script writing. This progress enabled calligraphic giants to appear like Zhang Xu and Huai Su. Together, they brought a brand new look to the calligraphic art of the Tang and Song dynasties.

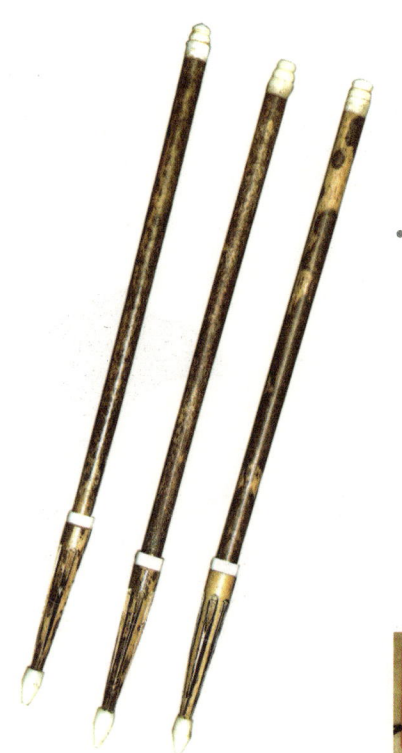

- **鸡距笔（唐）**

  鸡距笔因其形制似鸡爪后面的距而得名，其特点是笔锋短小犀利，缺点是吸墨性不好，易干枯。

  Cockspur Writing Brush (Tang Dynasty, 618-907)

  Because of a shape very much like cockspur it got this name. It featured a small and short tip that picked up little ink but dried up easily.

- **《自叙帖》【局部】怀素（唐）**

  《自叙帖》成书于唐大历十二年（777年），是唐代草书大家怀素的经典之作。全卷强调连绵之势，长锋笔的使用是此佳作的重要基础。

  My Narration (Partial), Calligraphic Work by Huai Su (Tang Dynasty, 618-907)

  This piece, done in 777, the 12th year of the Dali Period of Tang, was the best calligraphic work Huai Su ever did. Its flowing writing seemed to have a cascading effect. The long hair writing brush made this possible.

李白"梦笔生花"

李白（701—762），唐朝著名诗人，有"诗仙"之称。

相传，李白在少年时代曾经做过一个梦。梦见自己所用的笔头上开出了花朵，光彩夺目。这个奇特的梦让李白感到十分诧异。从此以后，李白的才思更加锐进，他创作了大量的不朽诗篇，成为举世闻名的大诗人。后来，"梦笔生花"一词被用来形容文人文笔优美、风格俊逸、文思敏捷。

"Writing Brush Blooms" in Li Bai's Dream

Li Bai (701-762) was the legendary poet of the Tang Dynasty.

He had a dream in his boyhood, as the legend says, dreaming that the brush he used blossomed with glorious flowers. This peculiar dream made him feel very suprised. From this moment on, his literary talents doubled, leaving one immortal poem after another and he was viewed as unchallengeable in attainments. This story was later boiled down to a proverb to describe a graceful and smooth style in which one writes.

- 李白像
  Li Bai

- 北京戴月轩精制湖笔
  Hu Style Writing Brush, from *Daiyue Xuan*, Beijing

宋元时期的毛笔

宋元时期，毛笔的制作更加发达，在种类和制笔工艺上都超越唐代。北宋时期（960—1127），宣州仍然是当时的制笔中心，但到了北宋后期，为了逃避战乱，宣州的许多制笔名匠逃至湖州（今属浙江省），促进了湖州毛笔制造工艺的发展。南宋（1127—1279）迁都杭州，其政治、经济、文化中心也都逐渐转移至江南地区。到元代（1206—1368）时，湖州成为继宣州之后的第二个毛笔制造中心，"湖笔"从此名扬天下，并成为御用笔。

Writing Brushes Made During the Song and Yuan Dynasties

Writing brush making progressed even faster during the Song and Yuan dynasties, with more brush varieties than those of the previous Tang Dynasty. In its first half, commonly called the Northern Song (960-1127), Xuanzhou was still the center of this trade. But at the end of the Northern Song, many highly skilled makers escaped from wars to Huzhou of present-day Zhejiang Province and this gave birth to writing brush making in Huzhou. With the relocation of the capital city by the Southern Song (1127-1279) government to Hangzhou, the political, economic and cultural center of the nation shifted to China's south. By the Yuan Dynasty (1206-1368) that followed Song, Huzhou had succeeded Xuanzhou as the center of writing brush making business. The fame of the brushes made there, commonly called the *Hu* style brush, became widely known. Emperors used the *Hu* style brush only.

- 竹管笔（宋）
Bamboo Holder Writing Brushes
(Song Dynasty, 960-1279)

冯应科、陆文宝制笔

冯应科和陆文宝是元代毛笔制造名匠，两个人并称为"冯陆"。据文献记载，冯应科制的笔妙绝天下，经常被列为贡品，与赵子昂的字、钱舜举的画合称为"吴兴三绝"。

Brushes Made by Feng Yingke and Lu Wenbao

Both enjoyed a big name during the Yuan Dynasty, often mentioned together as "Feng and Lu". By history books, Feng's products were made exclusively for the emperor's use. The brush he made, together with the calligraphic works by Zhao Ziang and paintings by Qian Shunju, were described as "three wonders" from Wuxing.

- 冯应科像
Feng Yingke

- 冯应科制笔（元）
The Writing Brush Made by Feng Yingke (Yuan Dynasty, 1206-1368)

- 陆文宝制笔（元）
The Writing Brush Made by Lu Wenbao (Yuan Dynasty, 1206-1368)

湖笔

湖笔的制作以羊毫为主，紫毫、狼毫并用。湖笔按性能可划分为软毫、硬毫、兼毫三种，可满足不同的书写需要。硬毫笔弹性好，笔力强，落墨劲；软毫笔含墨饱满，易于挥洒；兼毫笔刚柔并济，易于掌控。

湖笔之所以在元代时得到迅速发展，与当时文人的参与有很大的关系。元代著名的书画家赵孟頫是湖州人氏，他不仅在书法、绘画方面取得了极高的成就，在制笔方面也颇有造诣。他从小就和笔工相熟，并留意制笔技艺，多方搜集前辈笔匠的秘技妙诀，潜心研究，还将自己的制笔感悟告诉好友陆文宝，后来陆文宝成为当时制笔的名家。

The *Hu* Style Writing Brush

Most *Hu* style writing brushes took goat, rabbit and weasel hairs as materials and used them together. They had different degrees of hardness to satisfy different needs—soft, hard and medium. Brushes with hard tips produced elasticity and wrote vigorous brushstrokes; brushes with soft tips picked up more ink than other kinds and were good for continuous writing; while brushes made with more varieties of hairs than one had advantages of both and were more controllable.

Why did the *Hu* style writing brush gain a rapid progress during the Yuan Dynasty? Because of an active involvement from men of letters. Zhao Mengfu, a famous artist in painting and calligraphy, was a Huzhou native. He was also a skilled brush maker because when he was very young he hung around skillful makers and collected tips from them. Later, he passed his experience on to one of his friends, Lu Wenbao, who later became a renowned master maker.

• 赵孟頫像

赵孟頫（1254—1322），字子昂，吴兴（今浙江省湖州市）人，元代著名书画家。赵孟頫博学多才，能诗善文，精通诗文、绘画、乐律，尤以书法和绘画成就最高，与颜真卿、柳公权、欧阳询并称为"楷书四大家"。

Zhao Mengfu

Zhao Mengfu (1254-1322), alias Ziang, a native of Wuxing (present-day Huzhou of Zhejiang Province), famous artist in painting and calligraphy, a great talent in academic learning, poetry composing and essay writing, even in music. But the highest attainments he achieved were in painting and calligraphy, and this left him standing shoulder to shoulder with Yan Zhenqing, Liu Gongquan and Ouyang Xun as "the great four calligraphers in regular script".

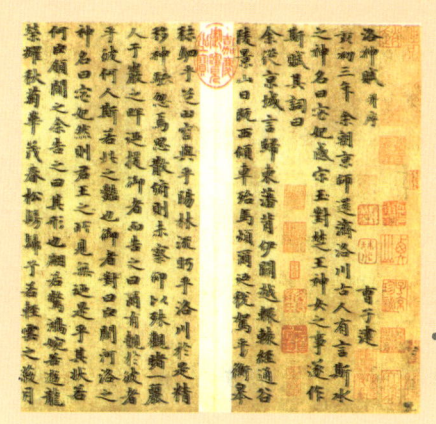

• 《洛神赋》【局部】赵孟頫（元）

For the Goddess of Luo (Partial), by Zhao Mengfu (Yuan Dynasty, 1206-1368)

这一时期，人们逐渐告别了跪坐的书写方式，改为坐在椅子上伏案悬腕书写，因此要求毛笔笔杆较短、笔锋硬中有软。在笔毛的选料上，除了传统的兔毫外，狼毫、羊毫应用越来越多，鼠尾毫、鸡毫等也有使用。在制笔工艺上，笔匠们制造出更加软熟、虚锋、散毫的新式毛笔"散卓笔"，笔毛中心有物的"枣心笔"及"丁香笔"等。

Beginning from this period of history people no longer wrote in a kneeling position but seated when writing, still keeping their wrists from touching the desk. This required a short brush holder and a tip of medium hard. Materials, apart from the traditional rabbit hairs, became diversified to include hairs from weasels and goats, squirrel tail hairs and even chicken feathers. Brush makers developed new types called *Sanzhuo*, *Zaoxin* and *Dingxiang* (lilac). All had new properties and a better performance. *Zaoxin* even had something hard in the middle of the tip.

- 竹管鸡毫笔（宋）
Writing Brush with Bamboo Holder and Chicken Feathers (Song Dynasty, 960-1279)

丁香笔

丁香笔是宋代的一种名笔，以精选的紫毫为柱芯，羊毫为副，以制笔名家张遇制作的最为著名。大书法家黄庭坚评价其"捻心极圆，束颉有力"。丁香笔自张遇之后就鲜见于世，其制法现已失传。

Lilac Writing Brush

A very famous variety during the Song Dynasty (960-1279), this lilac brush had dark hairs from hares for the major part of the tip and goat's hairs as a supplement. Among all, Zhang Yu was best known craftsman of this variety. To great calligrapher Huang Tingjian, this variety had unusual properties other varieties didn't have and was able to do brushstrokes other varieties couldn't. Yet lilac products were very rare and the craft got lost.

- 丁香笔选用的精品紫毫
  Best Dark Hairs for a Lilac Brush.

明清时期的毛笔

明清时期，毛笔的制造仍以湖州为中心，逐渐发展到杭州、绍兴等地。各大城市都出现了笔庄，专门销售毛笔，这些笔庄往往会挂上"湖笔"或"宣笔"的牌子。由于明清时期书画艺术繁荣，

Writing Brushes Made During the Ming and Qing Dynasties

The Ming and Qing dynasties still had Huzhou as the center of writing brush making business. The business had spread to nearby Hangzhou and Shaoxing. In many cities, shops in writing brush business appeared and most of them proudly had a

更加促进了制笔业的发展，毛笔的制作工艺也达到了鼎盛。

"大明万历"款五彩龙凤笔（明）

Polychrome Loong and Phoenix Writing Brush, a Royal Style during the Wanli Period (Ming Dynasty, 1368-1644)

明清两代毛笔的制作受到御用笔和官府用笔追求奢华风格的影响，注重材料的选择和装饰的效果，风格较为华丽，具有浓厚的艺术韵味。从笔头的选毫来看，皇室和官府大多选用貂毫、熊毫等珍贵的动物毛；从笔杆的质地来看，除常用的竹木管外，还有用金、银、瓷、象牙、雕漆、玳瑁等制成的笔

Hu or *Xuan* style writing brush signboard outside. Due to the booming business in painting and calligraphy, writing brush making was on a fast development track and the craftsmanship was on a higher level never obtained before.

Because of the orders placed by the royal family and government, writing brushes made during the Ming and Qing dynasties had a pursuit for luxury. Makers spared no effort and cost for the best material available and the most eye-catching decoration to go with. Most tips of the brushes for royal use had expensive sable or bear hairs. Apart from bamboo, the traditional material for brush holders, gold, silver, porcelain, ivory, lacquer, even hawksbill were used. The decoration on the holder and the cap was very eye-catching, with impressive carvings or precious things inlaid. The most expensive types included the black lacquer inlaid, carved lacquer, sandalwood, blue and white porcelain and famille-rose china.

More varieties never seen before appeared during the Ming and Qing dynasties for different needs in painting and calligraphy, under the names of *Doubi*, *Zhuabi*, *Tibi* and *Lianbi*, etc. Brush tips also had more varieties,

管；从笔杆的装饰来看，其雕刻和镶嵌异常精美，有黑彩漆镶嵌笔管、剔红笔管、檀香木雕笔管、青花瓷笔管、粉彩瓷笔管等装饰精美的笔管。

including the bamboo shoot, *Xiangpan*, orchid and gourd styles.

- 牛筋驼毛笔（明）
Cowheel Writing Brush with Camel Hairs (Ming Dynasty, 1368-1644)

- 木、玉、牙、角制笔管的笔（清）
Writing Brushes Made with Wood, Jade, Ivory and Rhino Horn (Qing Dynasty, 1616-1911)

此外，明清时期毛笔的品种更加丰富。制笔工匠根据书法、绘画的具体需要，创造出了斗笔、抓笔、提笔、联笔等新品种。在笔头的部分，捆扎出竹笋式、香盘式、兰花式、葫芦式等多种形式。

- 紫檀木嵌银丝大抓笔（清）
Narra Holding Brushes Inlaid with Silver Threads (Qing Dynasty, 1616-1911)

毛笔的制作流程
Steps to Make Writing Brushes

毛笔看似简单，但其制作过程却十分复杂，从选料到成笔要经过百余道工序。古代毛笔制作中最主要的工序有以下几个。

Seemingly simple, the craft was actually very complicated and demanding. From the material choosing to the final finishing there were a hundred steps, but the major ones being the following few.

选毫：将采集的动物毛全都放在砧板上，将无用的杂毛去除，收集剩余的毫毛。选毫是制笔成败的关键，因此要求极其严格，有"千万毛中选一毫"之说。选好的毫毛还要按照粗细、长短、软硬度进行分类，以满足制笔的不同需要。

Hairs selection: the selected animal hairs were left on board for further sorting; only the best ones were used. This step was crucial because it determined success or failure of the final product. "Using only the best of the best" was not an exaggeration for this step. Even those selected were sorted again by their thickness, length and degrees of hardness used for different varieties.

- 制笔的各种笔毛
  Hairs Selection for Tips

熟毫：将毫毛按类别浸泡在石灰水中，然后去脂、去腥，经过这种处理的笔毫有的毛色偏黄，有的发白，弹性增强，经久耐用。

"Cooking" the hairs: "cooking" meant to leave the hairs selected inside limestone water to remove grease and bad odor. After "cooking" hairs took on a yellowish or cream look but became more elastic and endurable.

- 熟毫
  "Cooking" the Hairs

水作工：这是毛笔制作中最关键的工序之一。将熟毫放在水盆内用牛角梳反复洗涤梳理，然后将毫毛制成片状，放在兽骨或压力板上反复地按压拉扯，使所有毫毛都整齐平铺于板面上，再按照所需笔锋的长度截取毫毛，其要求是"顶锋毫齐""锋颖齐""下根齐"，而且要求清洁干净，这样便制成了半成品的笔头。

Processing with water: this was also a crucial step. "Cooked" hairs were washed and combed repeatedly in water with an ox horn comb before they were pressed into very thin and flat pieces on a board. Then different lengths were picked out by needs. This was a very demanding step for every hair had to show very clean-cut ends and sides and free of dirt. By now, they were half-finished tips.

- 水作工
  Processing with Water

结头：这道工序是将制好的半成品笔头结扎。将处理好的笔毫晾干，按照比例搭配好后，用线将笔头扎紧缚牢。捆扎时用力要均匀，以防笔头变形。

Tip making: this step was to tie the half finished hairs into a tip after they were completely dry and sorted by a prescribed percentage. Thread was used, and the force applied when tying had to be even, neither too hard nor too gentle. Otherwise, the tip might deform.

- 结头
  Tip Making

蒲墩：笔管的选用和制作。笔管的材料以直、坚实、光滑润洁者为好。选好的管料经加工后，将两端挫平，再在一端挖出与笔头相配的笔斗，以装填笔头。

Pudun: *Pudun* means selecting materials and making the holder. Materials chosen had to be very straight, hard and smooth and shiny. After initial processing, the material was filed away on both ends. One end was hollowed to receive the tip.

装套：将制好的笔头和笔管进行装配，如有笔帽也包括在内。将笔头的底部放于火上烤热，并均匀地滴上热松香，使其渗入到笔毫的内部，这样毫毛才不易脱落，笔锋也更加锋利。

Capping: this meant to assemble the tip and the holder and a cap if there was one. The end of the tip was heated first on fire before receiving melted rosin until it went all the way down to the inner part. This was to fasten hairs and make the tip edge sharp.

择笔：将笔毫捻成笔头的形状，剔掉弯曲的毫毛，将笔头抹光，达到毛笔"尖、齐、圆、健"的要求。

Tip shaping: this step was to twirl the hairs until they adopted the right shape. Less straight hairs were removed while smoothing until the tip met requirements: pointed, neat, round and vigorous.

雕刻：在笔管上雕刻笔名、古诗词、工匠名字等，明清时还有在笔管上雕刻图画的。

Carving: this step was to inscribe lines from a poem or the maker's name onto the holder. During the Ming and Qing dynasties, a miniature painting was also seen carved on it.

- 择笔
  Tip Shaping

- 雕刻
  Carving

> 毛笔的种类

毛笔的种类繁多，且有多种分类方法。比较常用的是按笔毫软硬、笔锋长短、笔头用途等进行划分。

> Varieties of Writing Brushes

Writing brushes were in many varieties and the ways to classify them were equally many. Very often the classification went by the hardness, length and function of tips and the needs they were made for.

- 胎发笔（清）

胎发笔是用新生婴儿第一次理发剃下的头发制成的毛笔。胎发细腻柔软，中国古代书香门第很多都将胎儿的毛发制成毛笔进行收藏，以此作为书香传世的表征。

Fetal-hair Writing Brush (Qing Dynasty, 1616-1911)

Fetal hair came from the first haircut an infant had. These hairs were exceptionally soft and tender. Since ancient times scholars' families collected these hairs for brush making as a symbol of the age-old book-reading family.

毛笔的结构
Structure of a Writing Brush

毛笔在结构上分为笔头、笔管、笔帽三部分。其中以笔头最为重要，笔管装饰性最强，笔帽则属附件。

Structurally, a writing brush had three parts, the tip, the holder and the cap. Of the three, the tip was the most important while the holder the most decorative and the cap, just an accessory.

笔头是毛笔蓄墨和写字的部分，常用兽毛制成。笔头从上至下可分为笔根、笔腰、笔锋、笔端四部分，从里至外又可分为芯毫、披毫和副毫三部分。

The tip was for keeping ink and doing brushstrokes. Most of the tips were made with animal hairs. From top to the bottom, the tip had four parts: the root, waist, edge and end. Seen from inside to the outside, it had three parts: *Xinhao* (the core), *Pihao* (the outside hairs) and *Fuhao* (the hairs in between).

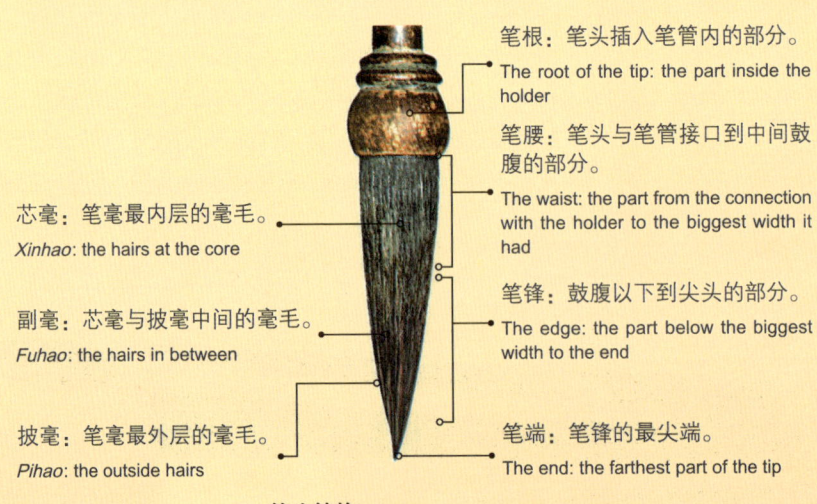

芯毫：笔毫最内层的毫毛。
Xinhao: the hairs at the core

副毫：芯毫与披毫中间的毫毛。
Fuhao: the hairs in between

披毫：笔毫最外层的毫毛。
Pihao: the outside hairs

笔根：笔头插入笔管内的部分。
The root of the tip: the part inside the holder

笔腰：笔头与笔管接口到中间鼓腹的部分。
The waist: the part from the connection with the holder to the biggest width it had

笔锋：鼓腹以下到尖头的部分。
The edge: the part below the biggest width to the end

笔端：笔锋的最尖端。
The end: the farthest part of the tip

- 笔头结构
Structure of the Writing Brush Tip

笔管也称"笔杆"，是手握书写的部分。笔管的一端是装连笔头的笔斗，另一端是笔顶。笔顶的样式丰富，有的呈球形便于手握，有的呈横截面状，上面有挂头便于悬挂。

The holder was the part for the writer to hold. One end was hollow to receive hairs while the other end was often shaped into, say a ball for easy holding, or a cross section with a hook for convenient hanging.

笔顶
Top

笔斗
Tip holder

• 笔管
Writing Brush Holder

笔帽又称"笔套"，是用来保护笔头不受损伤的工具。笔帽以竹质为多，也有木质或金属质的，现代笔帽则以塑料制品居多。

The writing brush cap was for a protection purpose, which was made with bamboo, wood or metal. Contemporary products are often plastic.

笔帽
Brush cap

• 剔红人物狼毫笔（明）

剔红又名"雕红漆"，是在器物的胎体上刷上几十层甚至一两百层的红漆，等累积到一定的厚度时描上画稿，然后再雕刻出花纹。

Weasel-hair Writing Brush with Human Figure Carved on Lacquer (Ming Dynasty, 1368-1644)

Carved lacquer had another name, "red lacquer", which came from the way of its making: applying dozens, even hundreds of layers of coats to the brush until the thickness was right to receive a draft before carving began.

根据笔毫软硬的不同，毛笔可分为硬毫笔、软毫笔、兼毫笔三种。

硬毫笔通常是用一种弹性较好、毛质较硬的兽毛来制作，常见的有狼毫、紫毫、鼠尾毫、鹿毫、马毫、猪毫、貂毫等。硬毫笔适宜

By different degrees of hardness, writing brushes could be categorized into three varieties: the hard, the soft and the medium that had hairs of different kinds.

The hard ones were more elastic, often made with tough animal hairs from

书写行书、草书，其特点是锋毫刚硬，弹性十足，落纸锋芒显露，枯湿燥润变化分明，写、绘出的线条刚劲挺拔，呈现瘦劲、锐利、峻峭之感。其不足之处是吸水性不强。

weasels, hares, goats, squirrel tails, deer, horses, hogs and sables. This variety was nice for running and cursive script writing, able to show the vigor needed and a nice variation between wetness and dryness on paper. The brushstrokes it did might look tall and straight, thin and vigorous, sharp and steep. But this variety had a disadvantage: it picked up less ink than other kinds.

- **紫毫笔（元）**

紫毫笔即兔毫笔，是由野兔背脊上的一小撮毛制成，因毛色呈紫黑而得名。笔毫尖锐刚硬，毫毛直顺。因受兔毛长度的限制，只能作小笔，缺点是不耐久用，容易秃头。

Writing Brushes with Dark Hairs from Hare (Yuan Dynasty, 1206-1368)

The name of this variety came from the dark hairs from hare's back. These hairs were hard, strong and straight but due to their less desirable length only fit for smaller brushes. Tips of hare hairs also had the disadvantage of being less durable and easily coming off.

软毫笔通常是用弹性较弱、毛质偏软的兽毛来制作，常用的软毫笔有羊毫笔、鸡毫笔、胎发笔、茅草笔等。软毫笔柔软灵活，富于变化，因此常用来书写篆书、隶书、行书或行草。软毫笔的特点是笔质

Soft-hair writing brushes had less elastic but soft animal hairs coming from goats, chickens, fetal hairs or reeds. This variety, as its name suggested, had soft tips that could easily change shape, thus very good for seal, official, running and

柔软，吸水性强，着纸润腻，使用时婉转、圆润、灵活，锋毫便于铺开，写出的字笔画丰满。由于其弹性不足，多用于书法和水墨画的大片渲染。

cursive script writing. It also featured a nice hydroscopic ability to leave very fine and well-rounded strokes on paper. However, due to less elasticity, it was used more in calligraphy and ink and wash painting than regular writing.

• 山羊毛
Goat wool

- 羊毫笔（清）
羊毫笔以上等山羊毛制成，多用青、黄、黑、白色的羊毛。羊毫质地柔软，吸墨性好，适于制作较大的毛笔和长锋笔。

Goat-hair Writing Brushes (Qing Dynasty, 1616-1911)
Most goat-hair brushes took good-quality goat wool as the material in different colors: pale blue, yellow, black and white. The hairs were soft and good at absorbing ink, ideal for brushes of larger size or longer tips.

• 狼毫
Weasel-hair

- 狼毫笔（现代）
狼毫笔是用黄鼠狼的毫毛所制，是最常见的硬毫笔。笔毫富有弹性，笔头有光泽，但毛质较脆，不耐磨损。

Weasel-hair Writing Brush (Modern Times)
Most writing brushes of this variety had hard hairs from yellow weasels, which were elastic and glossy but crispy and less endurable.

兼毫笔是一种混合毫毛笔，是选用两种或两种以上软硬不同的毫毛按照一定的比例组合而制成。兼毫笔将硬毫笔的弹性和软毫笔的吸水性完美地统一起来，可以满足书写多种字体或绘画的要求，运用十分广泛。最常见的兼毫笔有紫羊毫笔（紫毫为芯、羊毫为披）、紫狼毫笔（紫毫为芯、狼毫为披）和白云笔（狼毫为芯、羊毫为披）三种。

Writing brushes with mixed hairs made another variety under the name of *Jianhao*, which mixed hairs of different hardness as per a certain ratio. This variety was meant to pick up the advantages of other kinds to satisfy a much wider range of needs. The most common kinds in this variety were three: *Ziyanghao* with hare hairs at the core and goat hairs around; *Zilanghao* with hare hairs at the core and weasel hairs around, and *Baiyun* with weasel hairs at the core and goat hairs around.

- 兼毫笔一套（清）
  A Set of *Jianhao* Brushes with Mixed Hairs (Qing Dynasty, 1616-1911)

兼毫笔种类

根据芯毫和披毫的比例不同，可制作出软硬程度不同的兼毫笔。以紫羊毫笔为例，有九紫一羊、七紫三羊、五紫五羊、三紫七羊、二紫八羊之分。

九紫一羊是用十分之九的紫毫为芯、十分之一的羊毫为披制成，笔头偏硬，适用于精工书写。

七紫三羊是用十分之七的紫毫为芯、十分之三的羊毫为披制成，笔头偏硬，适用于小楷的书写。

五紫五羊是用二分之一的紫毫为芯、二分之一的羊毫为披制成，软硬适中，适用于小楷的书写。

三紫七羊是用十分之三的紫毫为芯、十分之七的羊毫为披制成，笔头柔软，适用于中楷、小楷的书写。

二紫八羊是用五分之一的紫毫为芯、五分之四的羊毫为披制成，笔头柔软，适用于行书的书写。

Varieties of *Jianhao* Brushes

Different ratios made different kinds of *Jianhao* or mixed-hair writing brushes. There were ninety percent of hare hairs plus ten percent of goat hairs, seventy percent of hare hairs plus thirty percent of goat hairs, half hare hairs and half goat hairs, thirty percent of hare hairs and seventy percent of goat hairs and twenty percent of hare hairs and eighty percent of goat hairs.

Ninety percent of hare hairs at the core plus ten percent of goat hairs around made a fairly hard tip good for writing smaller characters.

Seventy percent of hare hairs at the core plus thirty percent of goat hairs around made less hard tips, good for small characters in regular script writing.

Half hare hairs at the core plus half goat hairs around made medium hard tips, good for small characters in regular script writing.

Thirty percent of hare hairs at the core plus seventy percent of goat hairs around made soft tips, ideal for medium and small characters in regular script writing.

Twenty percent of hare hairs at the core plus eighty percent of goat hairs around made exceptionally soft tips, perfect for running script writing.

- **兼毫笔的制作方法——披柱法**

披柱法是在芯毫外披上披毫，是较早的制笔方法，目前仍是制造毛笔的主要方法。

Pizhu, Making Technique for *Jianhao* Brushes

Pizhu was to cover the core hairs with another kind of hairs. This was a fairly early way to make writing brushes. Today, it is still frequently seen.

根据笔锋长短的不同，毛笔可以分为超长锋笔、长锋笔、中锋笔、短锋笔等。笔锋的长短直接影响着书写的效果。

超长锋笔弹性最大，富于变化，可根据书写者的要求随心所欲地写出浓淡变化不同的字体。长锋笔笔锋细长，吸墨性强，写出的字饱满圆润。短锋笔笔锋粗短，吸墨性弱，写出的字苍劲，风骨毕露。中锋笔介于长锋笔和短锋笔之间，适宜日常写作。

Writing brushes could also be categorized by the length of their tips, the super long, long, medium and short. Different lengths determined the looks of the writing.

The super long was the most elastic and form-changeable, under different mood, writer could apply different forces with every stroke. After this was the long tip, which was very good for absorbing ink. The characters written with this kind of brush were well-rounded in strokes. The short tip picked up less ink but was able to give an old and weathered look through thin but vigorous brushstrokes. The medium length tip was good for everyday use.

- 长锋笔
  Long-tip Writing Brush

- 短锋笔
  Short-tip Writing Brush

根据笔头的不同用途，毛笔又能分出抓笔、斗笔、柳叶笔、面相笔、提笔、屏笔、联笔等。

抓笔的形制短粗便于把持，需要抓在手里写。其毫毛一般用比较粗硬的猪鬃或马鬃制成，这种笔是写仿宋字的最大的笔。

By different needs writing brushes had different kinds, *Zhuabi* brushes, *Doubi* brushes, salix-leaf brushes, face brushes, *Tibi* brushes, *Pingbi* brushes, *Lianbi* brushes … just to name a few.

The *Zhuabi* brush, as its name suggested, was held inside the palm and its hairs were hard bristles or horse mane. This kind was the biggest for writing imitations of Song-style characters.

Doubi brushes were for bigger characters in regular script, often made with goat hairs or whiskers.

Salix-leaf brushes got their name from their long and narrow shape like willow leaves. Their tip was long and thin, often used for small character writing or shades application to a drawing.

- 抓笔（明）
Zhuabi Brush (Ming Dynasty, 1368-1644)

斗笔用于书写比大楷再大些的字，多用长羊毫、羊须做成。

柳叶笔因形似柳叶而得名，笔杆纤细，笔锋狭长，多用于小字、铺染。

- 柳叶笔
Salix-leaf Brush

面相笔是用来勾勒人物线条或者渗线用的一种极细的毛笔，多用于壁画、人物画的构图。

提笔是用猪毫做成的专供写匾额用的毛笔。

屏笔是写屏条用的笔，比提笔稍小一点，多用长毫做成，属于大楷笔类。

联笔就是专门用来写对联的毛笔，联笔毫毛的软硬常常根据字体所需来配比。

Face brushes were for very fine delineation of human figures, often seen in frescoes and portraits.

The *Tibi* brushes, made with bristles, were for inscription on boards.

Pingbi brushes were smaller than *Tibi*, often made with long tips for large characters in regular script.

Lianbi brushes were for couplets on doorways and their hardness could change to follow the size of characters.

● 提笔（清）
Tibi Brush (Qing Dynasty, 1616-1911)

> 笔中名品

在毛笔漫长的发展过程中，出现了许多著名的制笔工匠，他们对制笔工艺的改良和创新推动了制笔产业的发展。他们从事制笔事业的地区也因此名声大噪，这些地区制作的毛笔成为人们收藏的主要对象。

> Famous Varieties

Over the past history many famous makers appeared. They advanced the progress of the craftsmanship and the place where they did business became famous. Writing brushes made in these places were collectables.

笔有四德

古人对选笔提出了四个标准，即笔的"四德"。笔有四德之说是由明代文人屠隆在《文具雅编》中首先提出来的，即好的毛笔应符合"尖、齐、圆、健"四个标准，即笔头尖、笔锋齐、笔身圆、毛体健。毛笔若有此"四德"，即便不是出自名家之手，也是上品佳作。

"尖"指笔毫的末端要尖利。将笔润湿后，毫毛聚拢时便可分辨尖秃。尖利的毛笔书写出来的点画自然、飘逸，气息灵动。

"齐"指将笔头用水润开，刮成扁平状

- 笔有四德
The Four Virtues a Nice Writing Brush Should Possess

后，笔毛须呈现出整齐均匀的状态。

"圆"指笔毫要圆实，无塌扁之处。这样才能保证书写时笔锋不会偏向一侧或随意绞转，影响书写效果。

"健"指毛笔笔腰应具有弹性。将笔重压后提起，随即恢复原状则说明毛笔有弹力，能够运用自如。

The Four Virtues a Nice Writing Brush Should Possess

Ancient people had four criteria when selecting a writing brush, which were described as "four virtues". This phrase was first put forward by Tu Long, a Ming-dynasty scholar, in his book *Wenju Yabian* or *Tools Used in the Study*. By him, a nice brush tip should be "pointed, neat, round and vigorous". In other words, the tip end should be pointed, the hairs neat, the tip waist round and the tip's body strong and vigorous. Any brush with these four, even not from a master maker, was a nice one.

"Pointed" referred to the end of the tip. After dipped in ink, the hairs should stay neatly together with a pointed tip. This pointed tip enabled graceful, flowing and lively brushstrokes.

"Neat" meant, when moistened with water, the tip came to show a very orderly shape.

"Round" meant round and solid hairs without irregularity in form. This round shape guaranteed the tip to not go astray when force was applied and no compromise in the brushstrokes' looks.

"Vigorous" meant the waist of the tip should be elastic and able to come back to its original shape when force was removed. This property guaranteed writing with ease.

李渡毛笔

江西进贤县李渡镇是中国著名的毛笔产地。据说秦代蒙恬改良毛笔制作工艺以后，当时的咸阳人郭解和朱兴由中原来到江西李渡一带，传授制笔技艺，奠定了李渡制笔业的基础。李渡毛笔的特点是选材严格，品种繁多，式样新颖，大小齐全，长短兼备，其毛笔精选各

Writing Brushes Made in Lidu

Lidu, a town in the Jinxian County of Jiangxi Province, is famous for making writing brushes. After Meng Tian reformed the brush making craft, people say, Guo Jie and Zhu Xing, two natives from Xianyang, came from the central plain to settle down in Lidu, where they invented new technologies and taught students, laying the foundation of the

类毫毛，有狼毫、紫毫、鸡毫、羊毫、兼毫等，笔尖丰硕圆润；装潢有黑、白、花等笔管。笔锋有红、绿、黄、白、青、蓝、紫七色，"纯净紫毫""五羊紫毫""墨宝""墨翰"等为传统名笔。

brush making industry in Lidu. Writing brushes made in this place featured rigorous material selection, more varieties to choose from, and a complete production line with different specifications. Their source of hairs was varied, hare, goat, rooster and weasel, either used alone or mixed. Their brush tips were rounded, full and hard, often to go with nice-looking color brush holders. Their brush tips, it was said, might be made in any color of a rainbow. Their dark hare, five-goat and jet-black varieties enjoyed a big reputation.

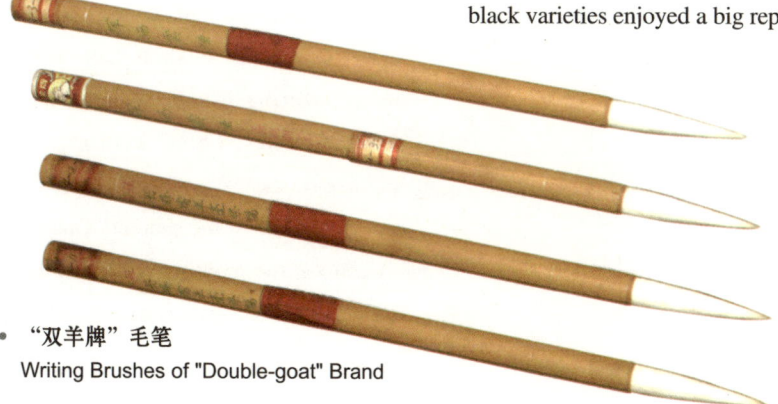

- "双羊牌"毛笔
Writing Brushes of "Double-goat" Brand

北京书画笔

北京书画笔因产于北京而得名，主要用于绘画领域。

到清朝中后期，北京的制笔业才逐渐兴旺起来，先后出现了吴文魁、韩殿安、胡魁章、陈富元等笔

Writing Brushes Made in Beijing for Painting and Calligraphy

Writing brushes made in Beijing are used mainly for painting.

Writing brush making made progress in Beijing in the mid or late Qing Dynasty, with famous shops named

庄。清末民初又陆续出现了王文通、青莲阁、李福寿、崔林元、胡文升、王德和等笔庄。这些笔庄以生产销售低档笔为主，是北京书画笔的早期形态。

著名制笔艺人李福寿潜心钻研制笔技术，根据画家提出的要求，并针对各个画家的绘画特点，反复试验，改进了笔胎的衬垫方法和原材料，制成了独具特色的书画笔。此后，李福寿不断精研笔艺，从而使得李福寿画笔成为畅销全国的名品，由此奠定了北京书画笔的地位。

after their owners like Wu Wenkui, Han Dianan, Hu Kuizhang and Chen Fuyuan. More shops came by the end of the Qing Dynasty, or in the early years of the Minguo Period. These shops as the early form of this trade in Beijing sold inexpensive brushes.

Li Fushou, a famous brush maker, dedicated himself to the craft of brush making. By artists' requirements, with their different artistic styles in mind, and after repeated experiments and improvements made on materials and cushions, Li Fushou successfully made painting brushes with Beijing characteristics. Later, with repeated improvements, his products became a hot item on the domestic market. Thanks to his efforts, the painting and calligraphy brush made in Beijing earned its fame.

• 北京书画笔
Painting and Calligraphy Brushes Made in Beijing

- 《蟹图》齐白石（近代）
Crabs, by Qi Baishi (Modern Times)

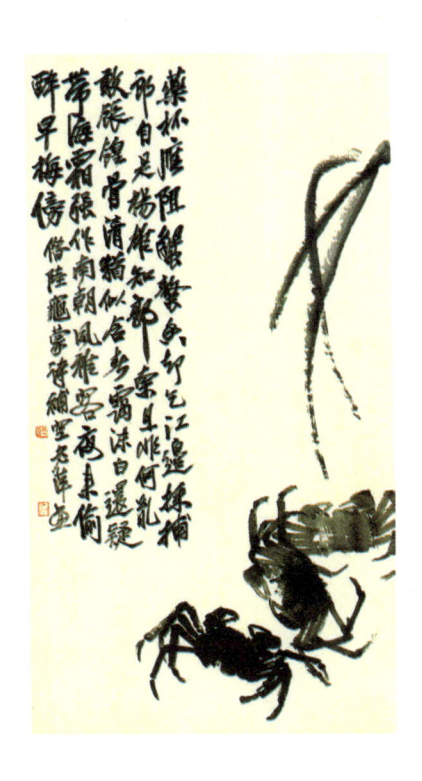

邹紫光阁毛笔

　　武汉邹紫光阁是一家有百余年历史的名笔店，其制作技艺源于江西临川（古代制笔业发达之地）。1850年，临川李家渡人邹法荣到武汉开设笔店。清朝翰林、书法家李端清（又名清道人）为该店题写"紫光阁"横匾。在之后的百余年间，这家笔店几经兴衰，分为了成记、益记和久记三家，到中华人民共和国成立后尚存久记一家。武汉

Writing brushes made by *Zou Ziguang Ge*

Zou Ziguang Ge in Wuhan is a hundred-year-old business in making writing brushes following the technique from Linchuan (a famous making place in ancient China), Jianxi province. In 1850, Zou Farong from Lijiadu of Linchuan came to Wuhan where he opened this shop. Later, a Qing-dynasty calligrapher, also an academician of the royal academy Li Duanqing, courtesy-named Taoist Qing, wrote for the shop its famous signboard. This business experienced ups and downs in the following hundred years, during which time it branched off into three: *Chengji*, *Yiji* and *Jiuji,* but only *Jiuji* was still in business at the time of the founding of the people's Republic of China. The writing brushes made by *Zou Ziguang Ge* with the best material and design have all the virtues a nice brush should have, having

邹紫光阁毛笔以做工精细，选料考究，设计美观，古朴典雅，"尖、齐、圆、健"而闻名于世。

a simple yet graceful look and being able to meet all the four criteria: pointed, neat, round and vigorous.

Song Brushes from Leshan of Sichuan

The *Song* brush from Leshan of Sichuan Province is for writing big characters inscribed on horizontal boards. It is renowned for the admirations of giants Su Shi and Huang Tingjian of the Song Dynasty (960-1279).

In ancient times Leshan of Sichuan was called Jiazhou. During the Northern Song Dynasty (1127-1279), Su Shi came to the Lingyun Mount in Jiazhou, where a pavilion on top of the mount had just been completed. Some monks brought a locally made huge brush, asking Su Shi to write a name for the pavilion. Upon

四川乐山宋笔

宋笔是一种写榜书匾额的大抓笔，产于四川省乐山市，因受宋代大文豪苏轼和黄庭坚赞誉而成名。

四川省乐山市古称嘉州。相传北宋时，嘉州凌云山新建了一座凉亭，当时正赶上大文豪苏轼在此游览。寺僧拿来当地特制的一支大抓笔，请苏轼为亭子命名。苏轼题写了"清音亭"三个大字，并当众称赞该笔为良品。时隔不久，北宋书法家黄庭坚也到嘉州游览，也用大抓笔留下"中流砥柱"的墨宝。此后，大抓笔成为天下名笔，后世誉之为"宋笔"。

the request, Su Shi wrote "the pavilion of pure music". He remarked highly on the brush's performance, describing it as a very nice variety. Before long, Huang Tingjian came too, who used the same style of product when doing a calligraphic work. After the two literary giants, this big holding brush became famous, known as the *Song* brush to later generations.

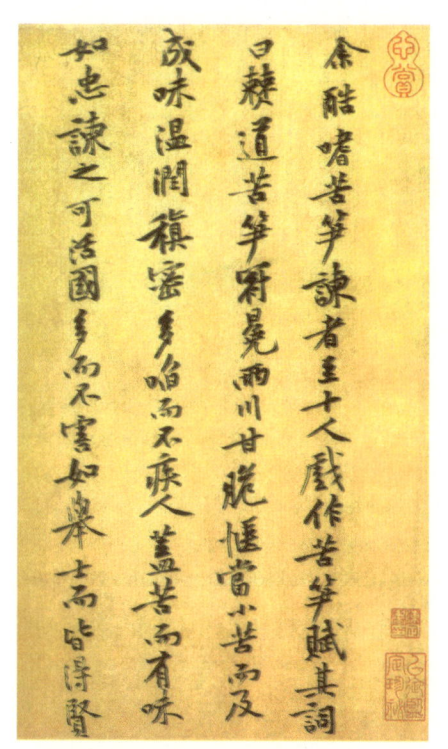

- 《苦笋赋》【局部】黄庭坚（宋）

Ode to Bitter Bamboo Shoots (Partial), by Huang Tingjian (Song Dynasty, 960-1279)

- 四川成都古玩市场里的各式毛笔

Various Writing Brushes in an Antique Market of Chengdu, Sichuan Province

韩愈《毛颖传》

韩愈（768—824），唐代文学家。他的文章《毛颖传》，采用拟人的手法为毛笔立传。在文中，虚拟人物毛颖（毛笔）被蒙恬俘获并献于秦始皇，被封管城，号管城子，得秦始皇宠爱，官至中书令。后来因为年老毫秃不中用，回到封邑，死于管城。文章以一支毛笔的产生、发展和废置为脉络，叙述了毛笔在历史文化上的作用和重要价值。

- 韩愈像
  Han Yu

- 《毛颖传》韩愈（唐）
  Story of Mao Ying, by Han Yu (Tang Dynasty, 618-907)

Story of Mao Ying by Han Yu

Han Yu (768-824), a Tang-dynasty essayist, wrote a biography *Story of Mao Ying*, using the name "Mao Ying" as the personification of writing brush. Mao Ying (referring to the writing brush), after being captured by Meng Tian, was brought in front of Qin Shihuang, the First Emperor of Qin, who gave him a title. Under the auspices of the emperor, he worked his way up to a high position until he lost hairs and became useless in old age. He returned to his fief and died there. The story spoke highly of the function the writing brush performed in culture and literature.

黄昌典毛笔

"黄昌典"是广西桂林市的著名笔庄，从清朝中期开始营业，以创店人黄昌典的名字命名。黄昌典毛笔代表了桂林毛笔制作的最高水平，曾有"黄昌典，买笔不用选"的民谣流传。

据记载，黄昌典是清代咸丰年间的秀才，擅书画，科举考试落第后开始经营毛笔。由于桂林野兔较少，所以历来制笔多用鸡毛。黄昌典为了改变这种局面，从北方购得兔毛、狼毫，并专门从华东聘请制笔名师到桂林制笔，由此诞生了黄昌典笔庄，享誉岭南数百年。

Writing Brushes Made by Huang Changdian

Huangchangdian, named after its founder, was a famous business in writing brushes making in Guilin of Guangxi since the mid-Qing Dynasty. Their brushes were the best in Guilin. People said, "You needn't pick and choose, every one of theirs is the best you can get."

Huang Changdian, the founder, passed the royal examination on the county level during the Xianfeng Period of the Qing Dynasty. After he failed the examination on the provincial level he quit the pursuit of officialdom, and turned to commercial business by doing writing brushes. Because Guilin had fewer hares, brush makers used chicken feathers instead. Huang Changdian changed this situation. He purchased hare and weasel hairs from the north and hired the best craftsmen he could get. His business enjoyed tremendous fame for several hundred years.

• "黄昌典"牌羊毫对笔（现代）
Huangchangdian Goat-hair Writing Brushes (Modern Times)

汝阳刘毛笔

汝阳刘毛笔产于河南省汝阳刘村，相传此地秦汉时期即已产生制笔业，至今已有2000余年的历史。东晋大书法家王羲之曾用汝阳刘毛笔书写《黄庭经》，觉得此笔洒脱流畅，婉转自如，赞其为"妙笔"，从此该地有"妙笔之乡"的美誉。汝阳刘毛笔的特点是尖齐饱圆，锋颖尖锐，犹如锥状，经久耐用，且性能刚柔相济，挺拔有力，运笔流畅，深得历代文人墨客喜爱。

Writing Brushes from the Liucun Village of Ruyang

The Liucun Village of Ruyang, Henan Province, is said to begin making writing brushes during the Qin and Han dynasties over 2000 years ago. Famous calligraphy artist Wang Xizhi of the Eastern Jin Dynasty wrote the famous work *Taoist Sutra of Huangting* with a brush from this village. To him, that brush was perfect, which he described as "something not from this world", so this village gained tremendous fame for many years to come. The brushes it made was of a very pointed shape and able to last for a long time. Their tips were strong and soft, able to give a vigorous and owing writing. Because of this, they won the compliments of scholars and artists alike.

- "满园春色"湖笔
  "Garden Full of Spring Beauty" *Hu* style Writing Brush

掖县毛笔

山东掖县毛笔始于清代康熙年间，一直以用料讲究、做工精细、造型典雅著称。掖县毛笔选用福建凤眼竹和湖南湘妃竹等名竹作为笔管，并以粤、桂的黑水牛角作笔斗，其笔头选用东北黄鼠狼尾为主料，佐以适量香狸尾、兔须、鸡毛、豹毛和石獾尾等细尾毛制成。

- 竹子——笔管常用材料
  笔管材料的质量也是影响毛笔品质的一个因素。
  Bamboo, the Usual Material for Brush Holders
  The material for the holder had much to do with the quality of writing brushes.

Writing Brushes from the Yexian County

The Yexian County of Shandong Province enjoyed a big name in making writing brushes with the best materials available, painstaking craft and elegant appearance. Their holders were made with the best bamboo from Fujian and Hunan and the tip holders were made with the horn of black buffalo of Guangdong and Guangxi. Their tips used weasel hairs of China's northeast, reinforced by a small amount from leopard cat tails, hare, rooster feathers, leopard hairs and badger tail hairs.

侯店毛笔

在中国历史上，河北衡水素有"北国笔乡"之称，此地是中国著名的毛笔产地之一，以在明清时期生产宫廷用笔著称。侯店毛笔的特点是选料精良，做工精细，所制之笔锋长杆精，刚柔相济，含墨量多而不滴，行笔流畅而不滞。侯店毛笔笔管以角、骨、象牙、红木等材质为原料进行精雕细琢，管身饰以龙凤、花草、山水等图案，增强了整支毛笔的艺术性。

- 鲨鱼骨、兽骨杆羊毫笔（清）
  Brushes Made with Goat Hairs and Holders of Shark or Other Animal's Bone (Qing Dynasty, 1616-1911)

周虎臣毛笔

上海周虎臣笔厂是一家拥有300余年历史的老笔庄，于清朝康熙年间在苏州以"周虎臣笔墨庄"的店

Writing Brushes from Houdian

In history, Hengshui of Hebei Province enjoyed a big name as the "Northern Hometown of Brush Making", and its products were exclusively for the use of the royal families during the Ming and Qing dynasties. The best brushes from Hengshui were made in a village named Houdian, which featured long tips and elaborately wrought holders. They could pick more ink than other varieties and the ink on their tips never dripped. The materials used for brush holders were expensive stuff like animal horns and bones, ivory or rosewood. They were often decorated with patterns of loong, phoenix, flower, bird or landscape to highlight an artistic taste.

Writing Brushes Zhou Huchen Made

This factory in Shanghai is more than three hundred years old, founded during the Kangxi Period of the Qing Dynasty. The best known variety it made was weasel hair brushes for painting and writing, with tips boasting of all the four virtues, pointed, neat, round and vigorous. The sides of their tips were sharp like a knife and this was for writing vigorous

- 景泰蓝羊毫笔（清）
Goat Hair Brushes with Cloisonné Enamel (Qing Dynasty, 1616-1911)

名创店。周虎臣笔庄以生产狼毫书画笔、狼毫水笔著称，不仅具备"尖、齐、圆、健"的特点，而且锋颖锐利，圆润饱满，刚劲有力，经久耐用，富有弹性。部分毛笔还以湘妃竹、红木、景泰蓝、象牙等多种名贵材质为笔管，精心装饰，观赏性极强。

brushstrokes. Also, they were elastic and endurable. Some of the holders were made with expensive materials like rare bamboo varieties, rosewood, ivory or cloisonné enamel, very pretty to look at.

毛笔的保养

一支值得收藏的毛笔，要很好地保养才能保持它的价值。如果保养不得当，可能导致毛笔损坏，影响毛笔的经济价值和艺术价值。

如果是使用过的毛笔，一定要将笔毫上的墨汁或颜料洗净，并及时晾干。若有笔帽，可在晾干后套上。如果是未使用过的毛笔，则无须清洗。

毛笔的存放有挂放、卧放、盒放三种方式。值得收藏的毛笔一般采用盒放，一般为一支毛笔或一套毛笔置于一个盒中。挂放和卧放适用于普通毛笔。

How to Take Care of Writing Brushes

A nice writing brush needs good care. Otherwise, they would be damaged and lose their economic and artistic values.

After use, they have to be washed clean without ink or paint left on the tip, then dried by airing and being capped. An unused writing brush doesn't have to do this.

They can be kept in three ways when not in use: be hung up, laid down or put in a box. Expensive brushes are often put in a box, usually, one box for one or one set. Hanging and laying are for common brushes.

- 毛笔存放方法之盒放
  Stored in a Box

- 毛笔存放方法之挂放
  Hung on a Brush Back

- 洗净的毛笔要用笔帽套好
  Capped Brushes after Being Washed Clean

Ink Stick

　　墨是一种黑色块状的研磨颜料,广泛应用于书写、绘画、拓碑等方面。墨的使用,大大改善了文字的储存条件,加快了文字传播和演化的速度,也使中国古代书画拥有了独特的艺术风格。墨作为文房四宝之一,为中华文化的传播做出了巨大的贡献。

Ink sticks are ink in solid form to be ground for writing, painting and rubbing. The use of it tremendously helped the preservation, spreading, and evolution of written characters, giving traditional Chinese painting and calligraphy a very unique and highly artistic look. As one of the four treasures of the study, the contribution ink sticks have made to the development of Chinese culture cannot be overestimated.

> 墨的历史

墨在中国的历史源远流长，从最初的天然石墨到人工墨，再到各种材质、各种形状、各种功能的精美墨品及现在所用的墨汁，中国墨经历了漫长的发展历程。

墨的起源

墨的使用可以追溯到原始社会，那时人们就开始用天然的有色

- 石墨
  石墨是一种原始的天然墨。
  Graphite
  Graphite is a primitive form of natural ink.

> History of Ink

Ink has a long history in China, beginning from their initial form of natural graphite to man-made nice looking products of different shapes and functions.

Origin of Ink

Back in primitive society people used colored minerals for painting and these minerals was the origin of ink. In 1980, the black-red mineral unearthed from a Yangshao Cultural site of Lintong, Shaanxi Province, proved beyond any doubt the use of primitive ink used in painting. The ink seen on turtle shells and animal bones with inscribed letters from the Shang Dynasty (1600 B.C.-1046 B.C.) was taken as the earliest mark ink left in history. Though such minerals differed a lot from the ink that appeared later, they met the basic needs of painting, and with them, primitive

矿石作画，这些有色矿石可以看作是墨的雏形。1980年，陕西临潼姜寨村仰韶文化遗址中出土的黑红色矿石，证明了原始墨在彩绘上的应用。商代甲骨上留有的天然石墨的痕迹，被认为是最早的墨迹。天然矿石虽然与后来的墨有很大区别，但已经具备墨的书画功能，原始人用它们绘出红、黄、黑、白等不同的颜色。天然墨包括天然产出的黑色颜料，如树木燃烧后遗留下的有机物炭质、烟炱、动植物分泌物以及黑土和有色矿石等。

西周时期，人工墨开始出现。据古书《述古书法纂》记载："邢夷始制墨，字从黑土、煤烟所成，土之类也。"邢夷是西周宣王时期人，这标志着西周时期开始人工制墨。由于人工墨在质量和数量上远胜天然墨，这使得墨的大量运用成为可能。人工墨的出现是墨史的第一个转折点。

people did paint red, yellow, black, and white colors. Natural ink included black, substances existent in nature like the organic charcoal from burnt wood, soot, secretions from animals, black soil, and colored minerals.

Man-made ink appeared during the Western Zhou Dynasty (1046 B.C.-771 B.C.) and the history book *Ancient Calligraphy* says, "Xing Yi was the first maker of man-made ink and he did it from black soil and soot." Xing Yi lived during King Xuan's reign, which marked the beginning of man-made ink of his time. Because the man-made ink was better in quality and larger in quantity, its popularity was a sure thing. Man-made ink marked a major breakthrough in ink history.

- 隶书"墨"字
  墨，从土从黑。
  The Character "Ink" Written in the Official Script
  Ink, related to soil, is black in color.

春秋战国时期，墨的使用已经较为普遍。同期出土的实物竹简、木牍、帛书上的文字，经考证有许多是用毛笔蘸墨书写的。战国文献中还记载了关于墨的使用情况。

By the Spring and Autumn Period (770 B.C.-221 B.C.) the use of ink was common. Many unearthed inscribed bamboo or wood strips or silks had characters written with ink on them by writing brushes. Some books from the Warring States Period documented its use.

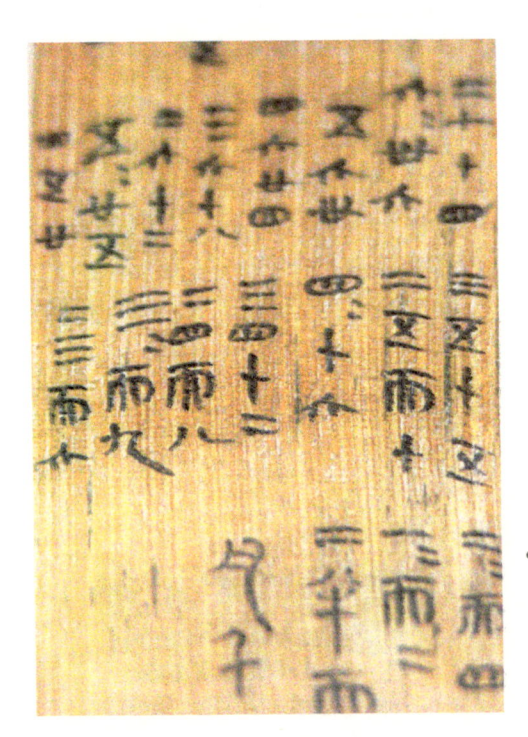

- 木牍（秦）
木牍上的文字是用毛笔蘸墨书写的。
Wood Strips with Written Characters (Qin Dynasty, 221 B.C.-206 B.C.)
The writing was done by a writing brush with ink.

与墨有关的词语

墨在中国古代与学问有关，因使用墨来创作书画作品的都是文人，所以与墨有关的词语多与文人或才华有关。如：

【墨客】指风雅的文人。

【舞文弄墨】指玩弄文字，含贬义。

【胸无点墨】比喻没有文化。

【笔墨功夫】指做文章的本领。

Phrases Related to Ink

Ink was closely linked to book learning in ancient times and everyone who used ink to write or paint was described as a man of letters. So ink was related to artistic or literary talents.

Moke, refers to scholars with a graceful manner.

Wuwen Nongmo refers to being unnecessarily frivolous with words, a derogative term.

Xiongwu Dianmo means unlettered.

Bimo Gongfu means the ability for article writing.

《泼墨仙人图》梁楷（宋）
墨是中国古代画家用来作画的最主要的材料。

The Splash-ink Immortal, by Liang Kai (Song Dynasty, 960-1279)
Ink was the most important tool to artists of ancient times.

秦汉时期的墨

秦汉时期，制墨业最发达的地方是隃麋（今陕西千阳）、延州（今陕西延安）、扶风（今陕西凤翔）等地。其中以隃麋产墨最为著名，后世还以隃墨作为墨的别称。秦代的墨多为墨丸，为团状或短小的圆柱状，使用时要放在砚台上用研石压磨。因此早期的砚台都附有研石，直到东汉时才出现能直接在砚上研磨的两头细、中间粗的"握子"形墨。

- **古砚和古墨（秦）**
  出土于湖北云梦睡虎地秦墓中的古墨残块，是目前可见最早的墨。
  Ancient Inkstone and Ink Stick (Qin Dynasty, 221 B.C.-206 B.C.)
  This broken piece off an ancient ink stick unearthed from a Qin-dynasty tomb is taken as the oldest ink stick ever discovered.

Ink Made During the Qin and Han Dynasties

During the Qin and Han dynasties (221 B.C.-220 A.D.) ink making was mostly seen in present-day Qianyang, Yan'an, and Fengxiang of Shaanxi Province, respectively called Yumi, Yanzhou and Fufeng in ancient times. Of all, the ink made in Yumi enjoyed the biggest fame. The name Yumi was even used to stand for the best ink. Ink during the Qin was made into small ball or cylinders shapes, and when used, was ground against a stone. So inkstones in the early stage often went with a stone stick for convenient grounding, a stick used to keep the ink from rolling away. This practice lasted until the Eastern Han Dynasty, when the shape of the ink took a change: smaller on both ends but bigger in the middle for easy holding.

During the Han Dynasty ink making was a valued trade. There were official posts in charge of anything related to paper, ink sticks, and writing brushes.

汉代时制墨业已受到重视，政府不仅设置了专门掌管纸、墨、笔等物的官职，而且还向文官按月发放墨块。据文献记载，汉代文职官员每月可领得"隃糜大墨一枚，小墨一枚"。

Each month, the government issued ink sticks to its civil officials. How many could they get? By history books, each got a big piece and a small piece per month.

"临池学书，池水尽墨"

"临池学书，池水尽墨"是一个典故，说的是东汉书法家张芝的故事。

张芝，擅长草书，有"草圣"之称。相传张芝练字以帛为纸，临池学书，将写过的帛在池塘里洗净后再用，久而久之，池塘水都变成了黑色。后人便将"池水尽墨"当作勤奋好学的象征。

After Years of Calligraphy Practice by a Pond, the Pond Water Became Jet Black

This is a story about Zhang Zhi, an Eastern Han Dynasty man.

The running script was his strength and he enjoyed the name "Sage of Cursive Script". When he was young he practiced calligraphy on silk by a pond, and every day he washed the silk covered with writing in the pond for fresh use the next day. After a long time, the pond water became jet black. Later generations took this as an encouragement for hard learning.

墨模

墨模是制墨时用来压制墨块成型的专用模具，多以石楠木、棠梨木制成，也有的以金属制成。墨模诞生于东汉时期，其出现为规模化制墨带来了可能，制墨业因此得到长足发展。墨模见证着墨的发展变化，许多珍贵的墨都是通过墨模制造而成。有的墨模本身也是艺术精品，比较著名的有"御制西湖名胜图墨墨模""御制棉花图墨墨模""新安大好山水墨墨模""御制四库文阁诗墨墨模"等。

● 古代墨模
Ink Moulds from Ancient Times

墨模发明后，应用并不多。从唐代到元代这段时期，墨模较简单，基本形式是多模一锭，即制作一锭墨需要多个墨模的配合。明代时，墨模得到改进，制模方式从多模一锭变成一模一锭，即将几块墨印合成为一个六面嵌套的总模具之中，每面上均有手工镂刻的纹样和文字。清代的墨模更加精美，雕刻技法高超，很多墨工穷其一生只能制作2～3副墨模。总的来说，明清的墨模艺术性很高，是制墨业发展巅峰时期的衍生物。

● 西湖十景墨（清）
Ink Stick with the Theme of Ten Scenes of the West Lake (Qing Dynasty, 1616-1911)

Mould for Ink Sticks

The ink mould was for ink clay to take shape in sizable production. Most moulds were made with expensive and very strong woods some with metal. The earliest mould appeared in the Eastern Han Dynasty. Ink stick production gained fast progress with the moulds. Some moulds, in themselves, were works of art. Among the best ones from ancient times are "the scenes of West Lake" "the mould for cotton growing for royal use only" "landscape of Xin'an" and "the mould of royal library for classical writings".

The ink mould was not widely used after its birth during the Eastern Han Dynasty. Even between the Tang Dynasty and the Yuan Dynasty the moulds were simple and needed more than one mould to finish. Things changed during the Ming Dynasty, when one mould was enough for one ink stick to complete, it's possible to make several sticks by a six-sided mould at one go, each side having an inscription elaborately done by hand. Moulds made during the Qing Dynasty became even more elaborate and impressive. Some makers might spend their entire lives on just a couple. It was a widely accepted belief that moulds were more artistically shaped during the Ming and Qing dynasties. They were a side product when ink stick progress reached a zenith.

- 棉花图墨（清）
Moulds Patterned with Cotton (Qing Dynasty, 1616-1911)

魏晋南北朝时期的墨

魏晋南北朝时期是墨发展的重要时期。这一时期，以松枝或松树树干烧烟制成的松烟墨完全取代了天然的石墨。制墨业最发达的地方是易州（今河北易县）。易州地区出产优质松树，因此盛产质地上乘的松烟墨。

三国时期，魏国书法家韦诞在前人制墨的基础上进行了创新，制墨时在原料中加入鸡蛋、珍珠粉和麝香等材料，从而使得制成的墨香味独特、光泽持久，具有"一点如漆"的效果。魏晋南北朝时期，墨的制作工艺已经成熟，贾思勰在《齐民要术》中第一次系统地记载了制墨工艺。

Ink Sticks Made During the Wei, Jin, Southern and Northern Dynasties

Wei, Jin, Southern and Northern dynasties (220-589) were crucial in the history of ink stick making. By then, pine soot ink from burnt pine branches and trunks had replaced minerals as the material. Yizhou (present-day Yixian County of Hebei Province) had more ink making activities than any other place in China. The soot ink it produced out of nice pine trees there was of the best quality.

Wei Dan, a calligrapher of the State of Wei during the Three Kingdoms Period (220-280) made a significant innovation in ink making by adding egg, pearl powder and musk to the material. Ink thus made had a very nice smell, shining and jet black in color. The making technique matured during the Wei, Jin, Southern and Northern dynasties. For the first time ever in history, ink making was documented by Jia Sixie in his famous book *Qimin Yaoshu*, or *The Encyclopedia of Agriculture*.

- 制墨图
  Ink Making

墨的制作过程

古代制墨全部采用手工制作，要经过炼烟、用胶、和料、制模、压模、晾干、加工等工艺流程，才能制出符合书写和收藏要求的好墨。

炼烟：取烟炱的过程。它是用不完全燃烧的方法从松枝或油脂中提取烟尘，得到松烟或油烟。

用胶：用胶的好坏直接影响着墨的质量，胶分为鱼鳔胶、牛皮胶等多种，用法各有不同。古人熔胶要求胶水清澈可鉴，这样制成的墨才不腻。

和料：先将烟料和胶融合熬制，再投入色素原料和配料，同时用杵锤炼，做成料坯。

制模：就是做模具，墨工先设计好图纸，再将木料雕刻成墨模。墨模的形制大小和纹理十分重要，各流派的做法都秘不外传。

压模：将初制墨锭压紧成形的一道工序。初制墨锭必须用一种叫"担"的工具压它，使其周围结实，棱角规整，纹饰清晰，基本成型。

晾干：墨成型后要平放晾干。在初期，墨要不断翻转，使自然拱翘的墨体自行恢复平整，然后将墨放入石灰，出灰的时间要求恰到好处，墨才能不软不硬。再经过扎吊，这对于温度、湿度的控制很严格，过分干燥或湿度过大都会影响墨的质量。

加工：晾干后的墨锭只是初具形态，表面有很多毛刺和疙瘩，还需要对其进行加工才能使墨的表面平整圆润。然后是加漆衣，这是一道刮磨工艺，而不是真的在墨的表面涂漆，其目的是使墨更具光彩。最后是描金填彩。描金一般以金色和银色为主，能使墨品光亮。描金的作用不仅是好看，而且有密封作用，使墨保持一定的湿润度。加工的最后一步是制盒和包装。根据墨的形状配制纸盒、锦盒、漆盒等进行包装，墨的制作就此完成。

The Process of Ink Making

Everything was done by hand in ancient times. Every step in the process, from soot making, glue application, materials mixing, mould making, shaping to drying and finishing, contributed to the quality of products which met the needs of writing and qualified as collectables.

Soot making: this was to get soot from incomplete combustion of pine leaves or grease.

Glue application: the quality of glue applied determined the quality of final product. The glue used was in different varieties like the fish glue and oxhide glue. Different types had different ways to apply. When melted, ancient people believed, the glue had to be a clear liquid and when applied thus it could prevent ink from getting sticky.

Materials mixture: this was to mix soot and glue with pigments added. The mixture was pounded repeatedly until it became a fine paste.

Mould making: by a pre-made design the mould was made out of wood and with carvings. The shape and veins of the mould were crucial and each school had secrets which never made public.

Pressing: this step was to make the ink paste into the desired shape. The pressing was done by a tool called "*Dan*" to make sure all the edges were solid, corners clean and patterns sharp.

Drying: this was to dry up the sticks. Repeated turning over was required at first and this was to get rid of uneven parts. After this, the ink stick was left in lime for a length of time. The time to be taken out was crucial for correct hardness. After this was the step of hanging, which required right temperature and humidity.

Finishing: dried-up sticks needed polishing to make surface smooth before they received a lacquer coat. Receiving a lacquer coat didn't mean as the name suggested, it was smoothening for a shiny look. The last step was to receive a gold or silver color to make the stick look nice. But there was something more to it: by sealing the ink from air it was able to keep the right humidity. Finally, it was packaged with paper, brocade, or lacquer containers.

隋唐时期的墨

隋唐时期，制墨技术已经十分成熟，这一时期制墨业空前兴盛，名匠辈出，制墨技艺高超，制墨中心从陕西地区扩大到山西、河北。易州（今河北易县）与潞州（今山西长治）是隋唐时期制墨业最发达的两个地方，它们最终成为隋唐时期的制墨中心。

Ink Sticks Made During the Sui and Tang Dynasties

By the Sui and Tang dynasties (581-907) ink making technology matured with master makers appearing. The places that made ink sticks were no longer limited to Shaanxi but expanded to Shanxi and Hebei. Yizhou, present-day the Yixian County of Hebei Province and Luzhou, today's Changzhi of Shanxi Province were famous two that eventually to replace Shaanxi as the center of this trade.

- 朱砂柱形墨（清）

朱砂墨多用于修改文稿或点校图书。

Cinnabar Ink Stick of Cylinder Shape (Qing Dynasty, 1616-1911)

Cinnabar ink was for book editing and annotating.

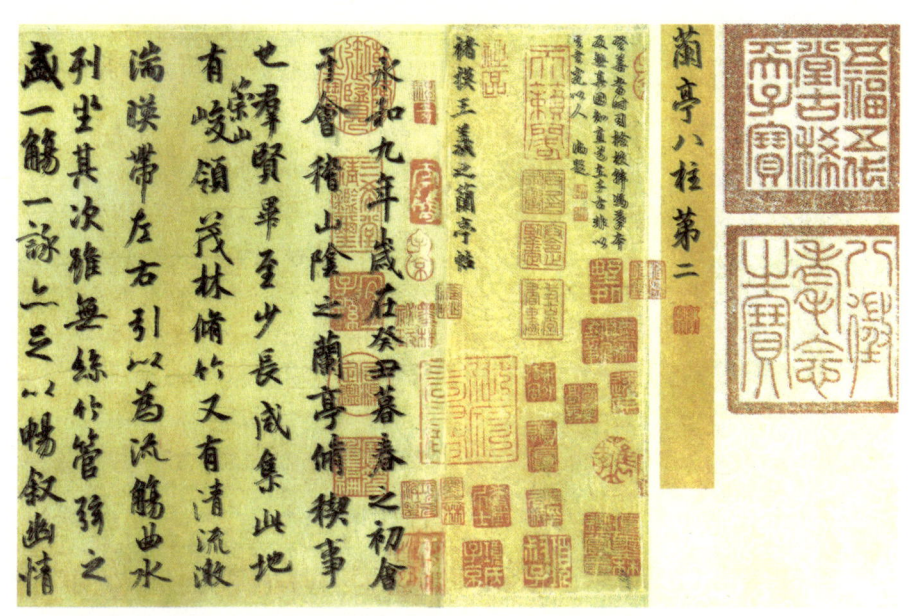

- 《兰亭序》（摹本）【局部】褚遂良（唐）
Lanting Xu, a Copy (Partial) Made by Chu Suiliang (Tang Dynasty, 618-907)

在成型工艺方面，墨模完全取代了手工捣杵，因此制成的墨更加坚实耐用，形状也更加多样。在装饰方面，工匠可用墨印将文字、图案印于墨锭上，这样制出的墨更具艺术表现力。

唐代时还出现了有色墨，以黄墨和朱墨最为有名。黄墨是用雌黄研细加胶合制而成，朱墨是将朱砂研细后加胶制成。有色墨多用于修改文稿或者点校图书。

由于唐朝后期北方战乱频繁，

When it came to shaping craft, manual work was replaced by moulding, therefore products were solid, endurable, and came in more shapes. Decorative characters and patterns could be applied for a better look.

In the Tang Dynasty, colored ink appeared, and the most famous were the yellow and red kinds. The yellow ink was made from orpiment powder with glue, while the red ink from cinnabar in very fine powder with glue. These colored inks were for book editing and annotating.

大批手工艺人南迁。在制墨名家奚超的带领下，奚氏家族举家从易州迁往歙州（今安徽省黄山一带）。歙州盛产的松树品质不凡，适宜制墨。奚超在此制作出丰肌腻理、光泽如漆的松烟墨，歙州也取代原料殆尽的易州成为新的制墨中心。

五代时奚超之子奚廷珪出任南唐的墨务官，对制墨工艺进行改进，在墨料中加入多味中草药，在胶料中又添加了漆，这样制成的墨质坚纹细、防腐防蛀，书写时流畅不滞，并带有沁人的香气。酷爱书画的南唐后主李煜喜爱其墨，赐奚廷珪以国姓"李"，即李廷珪，自此"李墨"名扬天下。"李墨"的

Due to frequent wars in the northern China, many ink makers escaped to the south, bringing along their skills. Xi Chao was one of them who moved his family from Yizhou of Hebei to Shezhou of Anhui. With the good-quality pine trees in Shezhou, Xi Chao was able to make the best ink, and Shezhou replaced Yizhou as the center of ink making. The pine resource was almost drained in the latter.

After Xi Chao's son Xi Tinggui became the official in charge of ink making, he innovated the technology by adding Chinese medicinal herbs and lacquer into the glue. The ink became finer in texture, mothproof and antiseptic, aromatic and smooth when being used. On top of these virtues was a very nice

- 李煜像

李煜（937—978），五代十国时期的南唐国君，世称李后主、南唐后主。他不仅精通书画，在诗词方面也有颇深的造诣，留下了《虞美人》《浪淘沙》等千古杰作。

Li Yu

Li Yu (937-978) was the ruler of the Southern Tang Dynasty. He was a genius, leaving behind quite a number of immortal works in painting, calligraphy and poetry.

出现，是中国制墨工艺趋向成熟的标志。

宋元时期的墨

宋代制墨工艺进入普及阶段，河北、河南、山西、山东、安徽、四川等地均制墨，涌现出诸多制墨名家，其中以歙州制墨最为兴盛。宋宣和年间，宋徽宗下旨将"歙州"改为"徽州"，"徽墨"由此得名。

宋代出现了以桐油炼制的油烟

徽州风光
徽州交通便捷，物产丰富，是产墨的名地。
Landscape in Huizhou
Due to its convenient transportation and plentiful resources, Huizhou is famous for ink making.

fragrance it gave. Li Yu, ruler of the Southern Tang Dynasty being an ardent painting and calligraphy lover, had a special likeness for this ink variety. He even went so far as to bestow Xi Tinggui, the inventor of this variety, the royal family name of Li. The ink he made was named the "Li's ink". The fine quality of this ink variety marked the maturity of ink making in China.

Ink Sticks Made During the Song and Yuan Dynasties

Ink making became popular during the Song Dynasty (960-1279), with many places doing it in Hebei, Henan, Shanxi, Shandong, Anhui and Sichuan. Many master makers appeared. Ink making in Shezhou was more active. Emperor Huizong of the Song Dynasty, during of Xuanhe Period, changed the name of Shezou to Huizhou. The famous *Hui* ink got its name.

The biggest contribution from the *Song* ink was the invention of soot ink made with tung oil, which exceeded previous variety in blackness, light reflection, permeability and stableness. The Song Dynasty also had a lacquer soot variety made from coal, grease and lacquer powder. This variety was jet

墨，其在黑度、光泽、渗透性、稳定性等方面都远胜于松烟墨。宋代还出现了以松煤加杂脂、漆末烧烟制成的漆烟墨，精黑发亮，用来作画经久不褪色。

black and shiny. Painting done with this ink lasted much longer.

When it came to ink stick making in the Song Dynasty, material selection was meticulous, shape, fragrance and color of ink stick should be of top quality. With precious items like borneol, musk and golden foil, Pan Gu of Shezhou made the legendary type with an improved formula. This type was described as "otherworldly", and its maker Pan Gu was deified as the "ink god" by literary giant Su Shi.

- 宋墨
Song-dynasty Ink Sticks

宋墨不仅讲究选料精、墨色佳，而且讲究墨香和形制。宋代名墨工张遇在油烟墨中添加龙脑、麝香、金箔等制成贡御墨。歙州墨工潘谷改进配方和造型，制成的墨被誉为"墨中的神品"，苏轼尊称他为"墨仙"。

- 苏轼像
苏轼（1037—1101），号东坡居士，世称苏东坡，北宋文学家、书画家。
Su Shi
Su Shi (1037-1101), a famous literary man, painter and calligrapher of the Northern Song Dynasty.

宋代文人不仅喜墨，也尝试制墨，关心制墨工艺，留下了不少有关墨的著作，如苏易简的《文房四谱》、晁补之的《墨经》等，对后世制墨工艺、鉴定与收藏墨都起到了促进作用。

元朝时，徽州仍是传统的制墨中心。随着油烟墨产量的快速增长，松烟墨开始渐渐被油烟墨取代。就工艺来说，元代墨模的雕刻风格更加浑朴雄健，制墨工匠除了追求精湛的墨艺之外，也更注重墨的艺术性。

Song-dynasty scholars loved ink sticks, and even tried to make their own. They put much effort into its technology. Some of their writings were devoted to ink making, Su Yijian's *The Four Treasures of the Study* and Chao Buzhi's *Ink Classical* being two of them. These books helped later generations' authentication and collection of ink sticks.

During the Yuan Dynasty (1206-1368), Huizhou was still the center of this trade. With the fast growth of ink made from tung soot, ink made from pine leaves lost ground. In terms of the craft, ink moulds exhibited a bolder and more vigorous style. Apart from continuous efforts for perfection, ink makers turned their eyes to artistic values.

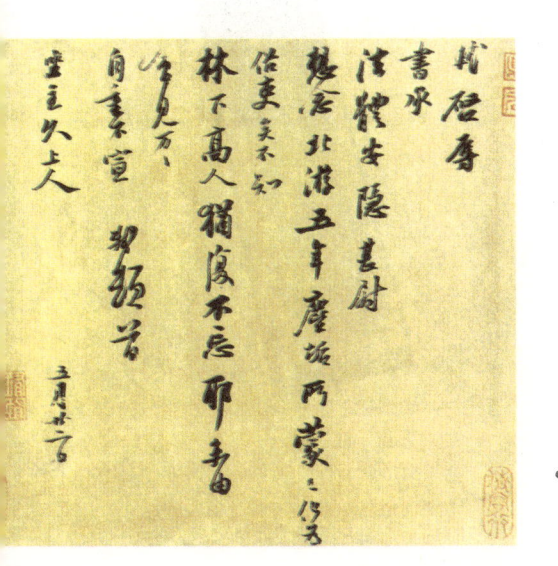

- 《北游帖》苏轼（宋）

Trip Made in the North, Calligraphic Work by Su Shi (Song Dynasty, 960-1279)

文人自制墨

文人自制墨始于魏晋时期的韦诞，他结合前人的经验，创制了"一点如漆"的人工松烟墨，开创了制墨新思路。

唐代著名篆书家李阳冰的自制墨被誉为"坚泽如玉"；宋代文豪苏轼自制墨采用高丽煤、契丹胶，而且自认为其所制之墨可与李廷珪、张遇之墨相媲美；此外，当时的陆游、黄庭坚也有制墨尝试。

明清时期，自制墨达到高峰期，如纪晓岚的"双弈道人吟诗之墨"、阮元的"研经室校书墨"、刘墉的"清爱堂墨"、金农的"五百斤油"墨、梁启超的"饮冰室用墨"等，各具特色，精彩纷呈，反映出当时文人的心志和意趣。

Ink Sticks Made by Book Readers

This practice began from Wei Dan during the Wei and Jin dynasties. From the formula of previous generations, he developed a new kind from pine leaves, yet being blacker and glossier. His innovation gave much for professional makers to think about.

The ink sticks calligrapher Li Yangbing of the Tang Dynasty made were described as "solid and shiny like jade". Song literary giant Su Shi made his from coal from Korea and glue from Khitan. To him, his ink was as good as the ink by Li Tinggui and Zhang Yu. His contemporaries Lu You and Huang Tingjian also made theirs.

This do-it-yourself game reached a peak during the Ming and Qing dynasties. Famous scholars like Ji Xiaolan, Ruan Yuan, Liu Yong, Jin Nong and Liang Qichao, all proudly made theirs to show their fine taste.

- 金农像
Jin Nong

- "五百斤油"墨
Ink Stick with "250 Kilos of Oil"

明清时期的墨

明代出现了规模较大的制墨作坊，制墨产业规模化、正规化，墨品的产量和质量得到提高，也促进了制墨品牌的形成。当时开墨坊、墨店的人增多，在流派上出现了"歙派"和"休宁派"。"歙派"以歙县的罗小华、程君房、方于鲁等为代表，制墨风格富丽堂皇，追求高古。"休宁派"以休宁县的汪中山、邵格之为主，制墨风格质朴，注重实用。

Ink Sticks from the Ming and Qing Dynasties

Workshops appeared during the Ming Dynasty (1368-1644) and their production became sizable and industrialized. Both varieties and qualities reached a level never obtained before. Brands appeared and more people entered this business. In terms of style, ink sticks had different schools like the *She* and *Xiuning*. The *She* School represented by Luo Xiaohua, Cheng Junfang and Fang Yulu, featured a luxurious and archaic look, while the *Xiuning* school with Wang Zhongshan and Shao Gezhi as representatives, boasted a look of elegant simplicity, mainly for practical use.

- 朱子家训墨（明）
  Ink Sticks Inscribed with Zhu Family Teachings (Ming Dynasty, 1368-1644)

- 五鸟叙伦墨（明）
  Ink Sticks with a Bird Pattern (Ming Dynasty, 1368-1644)

明墨的质量和品种较前代都有很大的提升，墨品更为坚细，锋可裁纸。明墨在造型、纹饰和包装等方面都更加追求美观，不再是单纯的实用品，很多都成为令人惊叹的艺术珍品。

Ming-dynasty ink had a much better quality than before, being more refined, and more clear-cut in shape, and "paper cuting" sharp on its edges. In both shaping, decoration, and wrapping, Ming-dynasty ink made a big step forward. They were no longer only for practical use but became collectables with artistic values.

明代徽墨四大家
The Four Best-known *Hui* Style Makers During the Ming Dynasty

罗小华

明墨歙派的代表人物，擅长制造油烟墨，他制墨用桐油并加入"金珠玉屑"等材料，使墨坚如石、黑如漆。罗小华曾得到嘉靖皇帝的赞赏，官至中书舍人。罗小华的墨品传世稀少，其主要代表墨品有"小道士墨"等二十几种。

Luo Xiaohua

Representative of the *She* school, a master hand in tung oil ink making. With gold and jade added to materials, the ink he made was as hard as stone and as black as lacquer. With the royal favor from Emperor Jiajing, he served as an official in the court. Of the few of his works got preserved, the best known ones are the "Little Taoists".

程君房

明代歙派制墨名家。他是歙墨的集大成者，被誉为"李廷珪后第一人"。他创造了漆烟制墨法。其所制之墨研后滴于桌面，反复擦拭都不见褪色，被赞"入木三分，超过墨漆"。程君房制墨质地优良，墨的品相出众，墨模的绘画和雕刻均出自名家之手，款式和图案都新颖精美，深得文人士大夫的喜爱，最有名的是"玄元灵气"墨。

Cheng Junfang

Another master maker in *She* style, the inventor of the lacquer soot, was taken as "the best maker after Li Tinggui". A drop of his ink on the desk wouldn't come off even if you wiped hard with a towel. Besides fine quality, the ink sticks he made possessed a very impressive look, patterns and inscriptions on the mould were done by famous artists. His works were very much sought after by scholars. His most famous product was the "Fundamental Elements of the Heaven and Earth".

• 程君房制烂柯图墨（明）
Go-chess Game Picture Ink Stick, by Cheng Junfang (Ming Dynasty, 1368-1644)

方于鲁

明代著名墨工，明墨歙派的代表人物之一。方于鲁曾是程君房家中的匠人，学到了程氏制墨法后自立门户。方于鲁制墨技艺高超，创造性地改革了不少制墨流程，其最有名的墨品是"九玄三极墨"。此墨代表了方于鲁制墨的最高水准，受到众多文人的推崇。方氏与程氏两位制墨大家的竞争，促进了明代制墨业的发展。

Fang Yulu

Another *She* style representative was Fang Yulu, who had served as a craftsman in Cheng Junfang's family. After learnt the skill, he left to start his own business. He made many innovations on the making process. The best known of his product was "the Nine Directions and Three Ends Ink", a man-made marvel of utmost quality to numerous people. The competition between him and Cheng boosted the development of ink making of the Ming Dynasty.

邵格之

明墨休宁派的创始人之一。他擅长制作集锦墨，得名师真传，制造的墨品貌繁多，质地如玉，极具艺术性和观赏性。其所制墨品都留有自己的款识，代表性的有"元黄天符""墨精""清都玉""功臣券""葵花墨""古风柱""梅花妙品""紫金霜""神品"等，现在传世的有"文玩""世宝""蟠螭"等。

Shao Gezhi

Founder of the *Xiuning* school, a master maker in making composite ink. His various products, smooth as jade, were all highly artistic and easy on the eyes. Everything he made bore his stamp. Among the preserved products are the "*Wenwan*", "*Shibao*", "*Panchi*" and so forth.

清代制墨业更加繁盛，以"徽墨"为代表的制墨业有了更进一步的发展，墨坊林立，墨在数量、质量、工艺技术、装饰、品相等方面均远远超越明代，达到了前所未有的高度。清代徽墨以曹素功、汪近圣、汪节庵、胡开文四大家为代表。

清代除了生产实用墨外，还生产观赏墨、彩墨、药墨等品种。

- 十色墨（清）

The Ten-color Ink Sticks of Emperor Qianlong, Bearing the Poem He Composed for Flowers (Qing Dynasty, 1616-1911)

"康乾盛世"期间，制墨工匠精雕细琢，不断推陈出新，集实用与艺术价值于一体的御墨得到发展。乾隆年间，御墨的制作工艺更是达到炉火纯青的境界。

The Qing Dynasty (1616-1911) saw a boom in business. The *Hui* style progressed further, surpassing that of the Ming Dynasty in quantity, quality, craftsmanship, decoration and looks. The best known four in Huizhou at the time were Cao Sugong, Wang Jinsheng, Wang Jiean and Hu Kaiwen.

Apart from ink for practical use, the Qing Dynasty had colored ink sticks, aesthetic ink sticks and medicinal ink sticks.

During the prosperous Kangxi and Qianlong periods, ink makers invented new types of both practical and artistic values. Ink making for royal use gained faster progress during the Qianlong Period.

At the end of the Qing Dynasty, Xie Songdai and Xie Songliang opened the famous *Yide Ge* ink store in Beijing to sell their signature product innovated from a traditional formula. Their ink liquid was easy to use and to store —

- 御墨（清）

Ink for Royal Use (Qing Dynasty, 1616-1911)

清末，制墨工匠谢崧岱、谢崧梁借鉴传统制墨的工艺和配方，创制了使用方便、易储存的液体墨汁，并在北京开设了专营墨汁的作坊"一得阁"。液体墨汁的创制是墨史上的又一次革新，给中国书画艺术带来了新的生机。

no grinding was needed. As another milestone made in Chinese history, this invention brought a brand new look to Chinese painting and calligraphy.

清代徽墨四大家
The Four Best-known *Hui* Style Makers During the Qing Dynasty

曹素功

清代徽墨四大制墨名家之首。他早年因科举失意而返乡以制墨为业，最初借用制模名家吴叔大的墨模和墨名起家，后来技艺日渐精良，名声远扬，墨业兴旺。曹素功制墨技术冠绝当时，常为权贵和名流定版制墨，最有名的是"紫玉光墨"。他还善制仿古墨，仿制了从汉代到明代的各种名墨，有"天下之墨推歙州，歙州之墨推曹氏"的美誉。曹素功还著有《墨林》两卷，主要辑录珍品墨和墨客题咏，是难得的墨史资料。他所开设的"艺粟斋"墨庄，子孙相传，历经十几代，绵延300多年，最后发展为近代著名的上海墨厂。

Cao Sugong

As the great master who topped the four, he entered this business in his hometown after he was frustrated in royal examinations. He started the business using mould and brand name of the famed ink maker Wu Shuda, thereafter, due to his excellent craftsmanship, gradually he earned his own name. The rich and powerful scrambled for tailor-made products. Of all of his works, the most famous was "purple jade and shiny ink". He was a master hand in imitation of ancient products, able to make replicas of everything from the Han Dynasty (206 B.C.-220 A.D.) to the Ming Dynasty (1368-1644). His legendary skill won him a tremendous reputation. He left two volumes of writing, which documented precious varieties of ink and poems and essays related to it. The two volumes of his made a valuable source for the ink making history. He also left a retail business, which, after the management of generations over the past three hundred years, developed into the famous Shanghai Ink Plant in modern China.

- 仿曹素功制集锦墨
Imitation of Cao Sugong's Ink Set

- 清代汪近圣制集锦墨
Ink Set Made by Wang Jinsheng (Qing Dynasty, 1616-1911)

汪近圣

　　清代徽墨四大家之一。他原本是曹素功"艺粟斋"的墨工，后来离开曹家，在徽州府城自立门户，开设"鉴古斋"墨店。汪近圣在徽墨中独树一帜，其所制之墨雕刻精细，装饰奇巧，艺术价值极高。汪近圣制墨，以小墨见长，著名的"黄山墨""新安山水""千秋光"等墨最具代表性。

Wang Jinsheng
Another one in the famous four, Wang Jinsheng had worked for Cao Sugong but later left to establish his own business under the name of *Jiangu Zhai* in Huizhou. His products featured painstaking efforts made in inscriptions and ornamentation and because of this his works had an

unusual value of art. Most of his products were small, the best known being "Mount Huang" "Scenes of Xin'an" "Light of Thousand Years" and others.

汪节庵

清代徽墨四大家之一，歙派最后一位代表人物。汪节庵制墨秉承徽州传统工艺流程，精选原料，改良技艺，所制之墨十分畅销。他创立了"函璞斋"，与曹素功"艺粟斋"、汪近圣"鉴古斋"并驾齐驱。汪节庵制作的墨有独特的香味，以"烟香自有龙麝气"而著名。汪氏的经典墨品有"兰陵氏书画墨""青麟髓墨""新安大好山水墨"和集锦墨"西湖图""古币墨"等。

Wang Jiean

Another one in the famous four, also the last of the *she* School, features an emphasis on traditional technique, rigorous material selection, and continuous improvement. His store enjoyed an equal reputation as those of other making masters. His products, however, had an unusual fragrance, described as "heavenly fine". The best known products of his were "Painting and Calligraphy Ink of Lanling" "Landscape in Xin'an" "West Lake" and so on.

胡开文

清代徽墨休宁派制墨的著名传人，他是清代制墨名家中商业成就最高的。他曾在曹素功墨店做工匠，后开设"胡开文墨庄"。胡开文制墨以集锦墨闻名于世。他精雕墨模，优选材料，其代表墨品是"苍佩室墨"。胡氏不但注重墨的内在质量，更注重墨模的雕刻和设计，不惜斥巨资搜集名胜古迹的蓝图，还邀请名家、名匠重新绘制雕刻，制出《御园图景》墨64块，墨中的图案包括圆明园、长春园、万春园、北海、中南海等园林景致。在经营上，胡开文非常有远见，他派儿子到全国各地销墨，积极扩大销售范围和影响力，在长江沿岸和东南沿海地区都开设了胡开文墨庄分店。1915年，胡氏后人所制的"地球"墨获得巴拿马万国博览会金奖，胡氏墨业驰名中外。

Hu Kaiwen

Famous maker during the Qing Dynasty of the well known *Xiuning* school, had the biggest commercial success among his contemporaries. After working for Cao Sugong, he left to establish his own business "Hu Kaiwen's". He gave equal emphasis on ink quality and mould decorations. His signature work was "Ink Set for Cangpei Studio". He invited famous artists to paint famous scenes of the royal gardens in Beijing. Through their illustrations he made the famous "64 Ink Sticks" to show beautiful scenes in the Summer Palace, Changchun and Wanchun gardens, the Beihai Park, and Zhongnanhai, all being the best known in the city. As a shrewd businessman, he sent his children out as salesmen so as to increase market shares and influence. He had retail businesses along the Yangtze and all over the southeastern coastal areas. In 1915, the ink stick "Earth" made by one of his descendants won a gold prize at the Panama Pacific International Exposition. Since then, the fame of his business became international.

• 胡开文套墨（清）
Ink Set Made by Hu Kaiwen (Qing Dynasty, 1616-1911)

> 墨的种类

墨通常可以按照用材、形制、图绘、用途四种方法划分。

> Varieties of Ink Stick

Ink can be categorized by materials, shapes, decorative patterns and use.

墨的用材

古代制墨的原料可分为基本原料和配料两类。

基本原料包括色素原料和连接原料。色素原料是将有机物经不完全燃烧，从烟尘中提取无定型炭粉得来的。松烟墨所用色素原料叫"松烟"，是用松树枝干和根烧烟而得。油烟墨所用色素原料叫"油烟"，是用桐油和少量不同比例的动植物油、生漆等烧烟而得。漆烟墨所用色素原料是燃烧漆料而得。连接原料是制造墨的黏合剂，它是墨块成形的主要材料，一般是用动物的皮、骨熬煮而成的动物胶制成，最开始制墨多用鹿胶、麋胶，后来慢慢流行牛皮胶。

制墨的配料是各个名家秘而不宣的独门秘诀。据统计，可用来制墨的配料超过一千种，常用的包括鸡蛋清、鱼皮胶、牛皮胶、各种香料及各种药材。

• 制墨配料珍珠
Pearl as a Kind of Material for Ink Making

Materials

In ancient times, ink materials had two parts, the fundamental and the supplements.

The fundamental included pigments and connectors. Pigments came from the charcoal residues from incompletely burned organic matter. The pigment from burnt pine leaves or roots was called "pine ash", while the pigment from oil was called "oil ash" which came from burning tung oil with a percentage of animal fat and raw lacquer. The lacquer soot ink came from burnt lacquer. The connectors meant adhesives to solidify ink, such as glue from boiling animal bones and fat. The oldest glue used was deer glue or weed glue. Later they were replaced by oxhide clue.

The supplements for ink making, a top secret to any maker, might total over a thousand kinds but the most common ones being egg white, fish glue, oxhide glue, perfumes and traditional Chinese medicinal materials.

• 制墨原料
Bletilla and Glue for Ink Making

按用材来分，古墨可以分为松烟墨、油烟墨、油松墨、洋烟墨、彩墨、青墨、茶墨、再和墨、药墨、蜡墨等。

松烟墨以松枝或松树树干烧烟制成；油烟墨以桐油、麻油、猪油等烧烟制成；油松墨以油烟和松烟混合制成；洋烟墨以煤或石油烧烟制成；彩墨以五色或十色颜料制

Differentiated by materials, ancient ink could be classified into the following types: pine soot, oil soot, Chinese pine soot, *Yangyan*, color, pale green, tea, *Zaihe* or mixture, medicine and the wax.

The pine soot ink was made with the ash from burnt pine leaves, and the oil soot ink with the residuals from burnt tung oil, sesame oil or lard. Chinese pine soot ink came from the mixture of pine

成，常用的颜料有朱砂、银朱、雄精、赭石、石黄、石青、石绿、蛤粉等；青墨、茶墨以油烟或松烟添加其他色泽原料制成，墨色含黛黑或茶褐色；再和墨以退胶的古墨、陈墨捣碎后再掺入新的色素和连接料重新加工制成；药墨以油烟和阿胶为主要原料，添加入金箔、麝香、牛黄、犀角、羚角、珍珠粉、琥珀、青黛、熊胆、牛胆、蛇胆、猪胆、青鱼胆等制成墨锭，可用于书画，亦可药用或外敷；蜡墨以蜡为黏结材料制成，是拓碑刻专用之物，携带方便。

soot and oil soot, while the *Yangyan* type came from burnt coal or fossil oil. Color ink used materials in five or even ten colors like cinnabar, vermilion, realgar, and ochre … The pale green ink and tea ink had, apart from pine soot or oil soot, pigments from other sources, thus in a pale black color. The *Zaihe* type, unlike other varieties, was made by mixing ground old ink sticks with new pigments and connectors. Medicinal ink took oil soot and donkey-hide gelatin as chief materials plus gold foil, musk, bezoar, rhinoceros horn, and antelope horn … This variety, besides painting, could also be taken as a medicine. Wax ink, as its name suggested, had much wax in it. It was a special tool to make rubbings off stone inscriptions, a variety very easy to carry along.

- 朱砂墨（清）
  Cinnabar Ink (Qing Dynasty, 1616-1911)

按墨的形制可以分为圆形墨、正方形墨、长方形墨、多边形墨和杂佩墨。其中杂佩墨是指模仿古代玉器、花草虫鱼、人物器具的形制所制的墨。

Differentiated by shapes, ink sticks can be classified into round, square, rectangular, multiple-sided and irregular, which meant fashioned after a flower, grass, insect, fish, human figure or famous jade object from history.

- 圆形墨、圭形墨
Round Ink Stick; Jade-tablet Ink Stick

"图绘"是指墨锭身上的装饰图案。按墨身上的图绘名目，明朝制墨名家方于鲁将墨分为六种：与皇帝有关的称"国宝"；与国家精粹有关的称"国华"；与神话有关的称"博古"；与人类生活有关的称"博物"；与佛教有关的称"大莫"；与老子、庄子有关的称"太玄"。

按用途不同，墨还可以分为贡墨、御墨、文人自制墨、礼品墨、仿古墨、集锦墨等。

Tuhui or decorations, referred to a painting or inscription printed or inscribed onto ink sticks. Ming-dynasty ink maker Fang Yulu classified ink sticks into six types by *Tuhui*: "state treasure" for those related to emperors, "national treasure" for those related to the nation, "antiques" for those related to mythology, "miscellaneous things" for those related to daily life, "great way" for those related to Buddhism and "supreme" for those related to Laozi and Zhuangzi.

- 十六罗汉图墨（清）
  Ink Sticks of the Sixteen Buddhist Guardians(Qing Dynasty, 1616-1911)

贡墨是古代地方官以进贡方式为宫廷生产的专用墨；御墨是皇帝专用的墨；文人自制墨是文人向制墨者定制的墨，在墨种、形制、图案、铭文上都可遂自己的意愿；礼品墨是制墨者出于商业目的而制作的墨，主要用于欣赏、送礼、收藏；仿古墨是用传世的古墨模制作的新墨，作陈设、观赏、收藏、馈赠用；套墨是两锭以上装成一盒的墨；集锦墨是套墨中的一种，为明代制墨名家汪中山所创，盛行于清

Judged by uses, ink can also be classified into tributes for emperors, for royal use only, ink made by scholars, gift ink, imitated antique ink and assorted ink.

The tributes were made by local officials for the emperor, while ink for the royal use only was ordered directly by the emperor. Ink made by scholars was customer-tailored in specified variety, shape or decorative pattern. Gift ink meant a present for a commercial purpose, mainly for display, collection, or appreciation rather than for a writing purpose. Imitated antique

- 金光悌进贡墨（清）
  Tribute Ink Sticks from Jin Guangti (Qing Dynasty, 1616-1911)

代，其特点是在一个主题下，设计出形制多样、装饰图案不同，但内容上又有联系的几十锭墨，组成一套，放在一盒里。

ink is made by using old ink mould, its uses the same as above-mentioned. Ink set was a packaged set usually having more than one stick. The assorted ink, a type of ink set, was an invention by Wang Zhongshan, but didn't become a fashion until the following Qing Dynasty. It featured different but associated patterns out of the same subject matter, usually up to dozens of ink sticks packaged in the same box.

- 胡开文制集锦墨（清）
  Assorted Ink Sticks Hu Kaiwen Made (Qing Dynasty, 1616-1911)

> 墨的收藏

中国古墨品种很多，在墨史上使用较多、地位较高的主要是松烟墨、油烟墨两种。另外，制墨名地徽州所产的徽墨也是墨史上重要的墨品，制墨名家大多也来自此地，他们制作的许多精美绝伦的墨是收藏的主要对象。

徽墨

徽墨是中国古墨中最有名的墨品，因产于古徽州府而得名。现在的黄山市屯溪区、绩溪县、歙县等地为古代徽墨的制造中心。徽墨的创始人是南唐制墨名家奚超及其子奚廷珪（李廷珪），徽墨历史已逾千年。

徽墨品种繁多，传统品种有漆烟墨、油烟墨、松烟墨、全烟墨、

> Ink Collection

Of all varieties, pine soot and oil soot inks were more used in history, thus more collectable than other kinds. So is the ink made in Huizhou for its unique position in history and many famous makers related to it. Many ink sticks they made are valuable to collectors.

The *Hui* Style Ink

As the best known variety, it got its name from the place it was made, Huizhou covering today's Tunxi, Jixi and Shexian County, all being active in the ink business in ancient times. *Hui* style ink was invented by the Southern Tang maker Xi Chao and his son, Xi Tinggui (also named Li Tinggui). By now, this style is over a thousand years old.

Even this variety has many types in it: lacquer soot, oil soot, pine soot,

净烟墨、减胶墨、加香墨等。现代徽墨在传统工艺的基础上不断创新，改良了茶墨、青墨、朱砂墨、五彩墨和手卷墨等品种，并开发了许多新品种，同时恢复了一些古代名品。

徽墨具有色泽黑润、历久不褪、入纸如晕、舔笔不胶、润泽生光、馨香浓郁、防腐防蛀、造型美观、装饰典雅等特点，深得历代书画家的喜爱。徽墨以松烟、桐油烟、漆烟、胶为主要原料，掺入二十多种其他原料精制而成。徽墨集绘画、书法、雕刻、造型等艺术于一体，使墨本身成为一种综合性的艺术珍品。

在徽墨发展的过程中，形成了歙县墨、休宁墨、婺源墨三大流派。三大流派各具特色，争奇斗派。

all soot, pure soot, reduced glue and increased fragrance. Modern types are innovated from traditional craft: such as the tea ink, the pale black ink, the cinnabar ink, the five colors ink and the hand roll ink. Some varieties that are lost in history are brought back to life.

The *Hui* style ink gives a very pleasant look, jet black, glossy and a dream-like effect on paper. It never glues the tip together. Also, it gives a fragrant smell, is able to withstand insects and highly decorative. For these features the *Hui* style ink has been a companion to artists throughout history. It takes pine soot, tung oil soot, lacquer soot and glue as chief materials plus twenty some supplements. *Hui* style ink sticks, in themselves, are works of art integrated with the charm of painting, calligraphy, carving, sculpturing and modeling.

The *Hui* style ink has three varieties, the Shexian variety, the Xiuning variety and Wuyuan variety, each highlights ink culture from a different perspective. The Shexian variety features an antique look, very fine in texture with very clear glue

- 耕织图墨（清）
  Ink Sticks in Farming and Weaving Motif (Qing Dynasty, 1616-1911)

艳，极大地丰富和发展了中国的墨文化，为中华文化的发展做出了贡献。歙县墨的特点是仿古隽雅，烟细胶清，多为贡墨及名家托造墨，以罗小华、程君房、方于鲁、潘一驹、曹素功为代表。休宁墨的特点是绚丽精致，饰金髹彩，多为套墨，尤其是集锦墨得到人们的钟爱，以汪中山、叶玄卿、邵格之、吴天章为代表。婺源墨的特点是朴实少纹，具有典型的民间艺术风格，深受人们的欢迎，以詹云鹏、詹衡襄、詹致、詹成圭和詹子云等为代表。

in it, often used as tributes for emperors and as gifts by celebrities. This variety had big names like Luo Xiaohua, Cheng Junfang, Fang Yulu, Pan Yiju and Cao Sugong. The Xiuning variety presents a very luxurious look in gold or silver, often appearing as a set much favored by many people. This variety also had big names, Wang Zhongshan, Ye Xuanqing, Shao Gezhi and Wu Tianzhang to name a few. The Wu Yuan variety had less decoration on it but was more antique looking, much preferred by people of higher taste. This variety has Zhan Yunpeng, Zhan Hengxiang and Zhan Zhi, etc, as representatives.

具有收藏价值的墨

现在存世的古墨已十分稀少，保存完好的古墨更是少有，因此古墨收藏越来越受到人们的青睐。具有增值价值的古墨多是出自名家之手的作品，目前存世较多的是明清时期的古墨。其中做工精细、品质优良、保存完好的宫廷御墨是最值得收藏的一个品种。

一般说来，实用墨的收藏价值远低于观赏墨，因为观赏墨的墨模多是雕刻名家精心制作，墨的图绘非常精美，具有很高的艺术价值。

品质优良的古墨经过千锤百炼，虽历千年但不会变质。通常说来，质地细腻、坚硬难化、胶量适中、墨色亮泽、清香弥久是优质古墨必备的要素。

Collectable Ink Sticks

Ancient ink sticks that have survived history are few, the pristine ones even fewer. So they are much sought after by many people. Of all, those from famous makers have more added value. Of all the ancient sticks we see today, most come from the Ming and the Qing dynasties. Those for royal use only, made with the best craftsmanship and still in good condition are the chalice to collectors.

Usually, ink for practical use is less valuable than the ink for appreciation because the later often came from moulds made by famous artists with artistic decoration.

A nice antique ink stick will last for a thousand years without decay. Such an ink stick often features a fine texture, solid, hard and difficult to dissolve, having glossy looks and a pleasant smell.

• 富贵图墨（清）
Ink Sticks in Wealth and Rank Motif (Qing Dynasty, 1616-1911)

墨的保养

墨无论是松烟墨，还是油烟墨，都是用胶黏合在一起的，因此既怕受潮霉烂，又怕干燥爆裂。所以，防潮、防干燥是长期保存古墨最重要的两点。刚收藏的墨，应用纸包起来封好，平放在盒子中，再将墨盒挂于通风阴凉处，避免墨与潮湿空气直接接触。

如果古墨存放不当，很可能出现受潮、断裂、弯曲等问题，这时就需要对其进行保养。古墨通常选择在最干燥的季节进行保养。

对于已严重受潮、生霉斑的古墨，不要急于除霉斑，应当先去湿。具体方法是先用绵纸将墨锭包封好，放置在生石灰中，过十余天取出，墨中的潮气便会去掉。再用软毛刷子或软纸擦去霉斑。

断裂的古墨可以用磨的浓墨做黏合剂，将断块黏合起来。

墨锭变弯曲可能是因为放置方法不正确，注意不能用力扳、压、敲墨锭。正确的补救方法是用纸把墨包封好，将弯突的一方向上，平放好，在上面压上一本不太重的书，过些日子再加重，时日一久，墨就会矫正过来。

The Keeping of Ink Sticks

Both the pine soot and oil soot ink sticks have glue in them and because of the glue they easily go moldy and are likely affected by dampness. They may also crack from excessive dryness. Keeping them from dampness and dryness is crucial. A new ink stick should be wrapped in paper before being placed flat inside a box in a shady and ventilated place. This is to keep the ink out of direct contact with wet air.

Left in poor condition antique ink sticks may get affected by dampness, break or warp. If this happens repairing is necessary, often done in a dry season.

Heavily moldy ones have to be rid of wet before removing the mildew. The right way is to wrap the ink in tissue paper before left in lime for ten days. By then, humidity is gone. Use very soft brushes or tissue paper to wipe off the mildew.

Broken pieces can be glued back together with thick ink juice.

A warped ink stick may come from incorrect placement. No force should be applied to correction either by pressing, bending or knocking. The correct way is to wrap it with paper and leave it flat with the bending side on top, put some weight, say a book, something not too heavy, on it and after days increase the weight. After a period of time the warp will be gone.

纸
Paper

　　文房四宝中的"纸"是指书画用纸，即宜用毛笔写字或作画的纸。造纸术与火药、指南针、印刷术合称为中国古代科学技术的四大发明，为人类文明的传播做出了巨大的贡献。纸的出现，不仅使人们拥有了轻巧方便的书写材料，更成就了中国传统书画艺术。在中国造纸历史中，也产生了许多精美的加工纸，具有极高的观赏价值和艺术价值。

Paper here refers to the paper on which calligraphy or painting or writing is done with a writing brush. Papermaking, together with gunpowder, the compass and printing are called "the four significant inventions the Chinese nation made in ancient history". Papermaking made a huge contribution to the spreading of human civilization. As a writing material in light weight and easy to carny along, paper parented Chinese painting and calligraphy. Apart from the paper for practical needs, some with high artistic value was invented for appreciation.

> 纸的历史

纸虽然是文房四宝中出现最晚的，但是它为中国传统书画艺术带来的翻天覆地的变化，是其余三宝无法企及的。纸在几千年的发展历程中，不断改进技术，推陈出新，出现了一批又一批各具特色的产品，其中不乏具有较高的艺术价值的精美纸笺。

纸的发明

中国历来就有蔡伦造纸的说法。据《后汉书》记载，东汉元兴元年（105年），当时负责制造宫廷御用器具的官员蔡伦，经过潜心研究，发明了造纸术，生产出新的书写材料"蔡侯纸"。但是考古发现表明，纸的诞生远早于蔡伦生活的年代，所以现代学者认为蔡伦只是造纸术的改良者。

> History of Paper

Though being the latest to appear among the four treasures of the study, paper made a change in painting and calligraphy unmatched by any other. During its several thousand years of history, with its making technology improved time and again, new varieties appeared, some being just works of art.

• 蔡伦像
Cai Lun

在纸产生之前，人们所使用的书写材料是竹简和绢帛。竹简是将若干竹片或木片用绳穿系而成，无论是书写、阅读还是搬运，都十分笨重；而绢帛则非常珍贵，无法普及。从考古出土的资料来看，纸应该诞生于秦汉时期。1957年在陕西西安东郊灞桥附近的一座西汉墓中，出土了一批"灞桥纸"。这些纸制作于西汉武帝时期，纤维束较

- 竹简（秦）
竹简是由竹片或木片穿系而成，体积大，在纸出现之前是主要的书写材料。

Bamboo Slips (Qin Dynasty, 221 B.C.-206 B.C.)

Bamboo slips are made by stringing together a batch of wood or bamboo slips and they are bulky. Before the invention of paper they were the main writing material.

Invention of Paper

Papermaking is an invention credited to Cai Lun. By *Hou Han Shu* or *History of Late Han*, in the first year of Yuanxing, the Eastern Han Dynasty (105), civil official Cai Lun in charge of the supplies for the royal family invented papermaking and the paper he made was named Cai Lun paper. However, archeological finds challenged this saying, suggesting papermaking was much earlier than Cai Lun's time. Cai Lun, to some contemporary scholars, simply improved the technology.

People wrote on silk or bamboo slips before paper was invented. Bamboo slips were slips bound by a thread, very cumbersome for either transportation or use, while silk was expensive, beyond many people's means. From archeological finds papermaking should have happened during the Qin or Han dynasties (221 B.C.-220 A.D.). In 1957, archeologists unearthed some paper from a Western Han tomb in the eastern suburb of Xi'an. That paper in a pale yellowish color, called Baqiao paper, was made during Emperor Wu's time and contained fiber in disarray. It was exclusively used for wrapping burial objects. Later, in Gansu,

多，交织不匀，呈浅黄色，专门用来包裹陪葬物品。后来甘肃省境内又陆续出土了"马圈湾纸""放马滩纸"。经考证，这些古纸的时间比"蔡侯纸"早了100—300年。

more ancient paper called by historians as Majuanwan and Fangmatan paper was discovered. Studies have proved they were earlier than Cai Lun's time by 100 to 300 years.

- 帛书（汉）

绢帛是丝织品，成本高，在纸出现之前是珍贵的书写材料。
Silk Book (Han Dynasty, 206 B.C.-220 A.D.)
Silk as an expensive stuff was used for writing before paper was invented.

早期纸的制作以麻为主要原料，制浆主要用石灰水，所制的纸颜色蜡黄，质量不高。经蔡伦改进

Paper was made from hemp in the early days, which was pulped by lime water and this explained why paper so made was yellowish and of low quality.

- 早期写有汉字的纸（汉）

造纸术在东汉时有了技术突破，但在发展初期并没有完全取代竹简和绢帛，而是有一个纸简并存的过渡时期。
Paper with Written Characters (Han Dynasty, 206 B.C.-220 A.D.)
Although a breakthrough was made during the Eastern Han Dynasty, paper was not widespread enough to replace expensive stuff like silk or cumbersome bamboo slips. For a period of history they co-existed.

后的纸以树皮、碎布、麻头、旧渔网为原料，经过细致的加工，生产出来的纸颜色较白，质地坚韧。蔡伦对纸的改进做出了卓越的贡献，完成了造纸术的改革和飞跃，为以后印刷创造了物质条件。

After Cai Lun's improvement the range of materials became wider, tree bark, cloth or hemp bits, even fishing net were used. After being processed by an improved technology the paper made was whiter and stronger than before. Cai Lun was a significant improver by revolutionizing the making technology, which made a necessary condition for print.

蔡伦造纸术

在蔡伦之前，纸的制作技术粗糙，经过蔡伦的改良后，造纸术得到广泛推广，并制造出质量更好的纸。

蔡伦改进造纸术后造纸的基本过程是：把渔网、麻头、破布、树皮等原料先用水浸，然后用斧头切碎，用水洗涤，再用草木灰水浸透并加以蒸煮，然后用清水漂洗后捣碎，再用水配成纸浆，用纸模过滤纸浆，再经过脱水、干燥、抄纸等工序，纸就制造出来了。

蔡伦造纸术相比之前的造纸有了三大进步：一是造纸原料来源拓宽；二是造纸过程增加，分工更细致；三是用草木灰水取代石灰水，草木灰水碱性更强，造出的纸颜色更白。

Cai Lun's Papermaking Technology

Before Cai Lun, the technology of papermaking was coarse. After he improved it, the paper was in a much better quality.

The improved workflow was this: first, soak old fishing net, bits of hemp and cloth and tree bark with water, cut them into very small pieces with axes, and wash them before soaking them again but this time, with plant ash water; steam them, rinse them clean, pound them into a pulp with water added, filter with a paper mould, then, after dehydration, drying and peeling, paper was made.

Compared with previous one, this improved technology had three major advantages: a wider range of material source, more steps added to make the procedure more professional and more specific, and replacing the lime water with plant ash water, which contained more alkali to make the paper whiter.

•《天工开物》中的造纸图 宋应星（明）
Papermaking, *Tiangong Kaiwu* or *The Exploitation of the Works of Nature*, by Song Yingxing (Ming Dynasty, 1368-1644)

造纸术的传播

中国造纸术首先传入朝鲜和越南,之后由朝鲜传到了日本。中国的造纸技术也传播到了中亚的一些国家,并通过贸易传播到了印度。

唐朝(618—907)时,与海外的频繁交往使造纸术传入阿拉伯,到10世纪造纸技术又传到了叙利亚、埃及与摩洛哥。

欧洲人是通过阿拉伯人了解造纸技术的。12世纪,阿拉伯人在西班牙建立了欧洲第一个造纸场。1276年,意大利第一家造纸场建成。14世纪,法国建立造纸场,当时法国造纸不仅供应本国,还向德国出口。14世纪末,德国掌握了造纸术。15世纪,英国建立了自己的造纸厂。到了17世纪,欧洲主要国家都掌握了造纸术。

新航线开辟后,西班牙人将造纸术带到美洲。墨西哥造纸始于16世纪。美国在17世纪建立了第一家造纸厂。到19世纪,中国的造纸术已传遍世界五大洲。

Spreading of the Papermaking Technology

First, Chinese papermaking technology spread to the Korea and Vietnam, then, via the Korea to Japan. It also went to central Asia and India through trading activities.

During the Tang Dynasty (618-907), contacts with foreign nations increased, which brought papermaking technology to Arab, then, during the 10th century, to Syria, Egypt and Morocco.

Europeans learnt this technology through Arabians. During the 12th century Arabians set up in Spain the first paper mill Europeans ever had in history. In 1276 Italians had their first. France had theirs during the 14th century. The paper it made was even exported to Germany, who learnt this technique in the late 14th century. The British had their paper mill in the 15th century and by the 17th century, all major European countries had theirs.

After the navigation route to America was opened, Spanish people brought this technology to America. Mexico began to make paper during the 16th century, and the United States, in the 17th century. By the 19th century, papermaking technology from China was seen all over the world.

魏晋南北朝时期的纸

魏晋南北朝时期，竹简、绢帛退出历史舞台，纸正式成为主要的书写材料。与汉代相比，魏晋南北朝的纸产地范围更广，产量大幅度提高，造纸技术也进一步提升。制纸中心从河南洛阳向全国扩展，形成了南北遍布的新格局，一些边远地区也建立起了纸坊，发展造纸业。

魏晋南北朝时期，纸的品种不断丰富，左伯纸、麻纸、黄麻纸、藤纸、银光纸是这一时期的著名纸品。

左伯纸是三国时期曹魏东莱（今山东莱州）人左伯所制。左伯

- 麻纸《平复贴》【局部】陆机（晋）
  Pingfu Tie, (Partial) Calligraphic Work on Hemp Paper, by Lu Ji, (Jin Dynasty, 265-420)

The Paper Made During the Wei, Jin, Southern and Northern Dynasties

Bamboo slips and silk for writing were replaced by paper during the Wei, Jin, Southern and Northern dynasties (220-589). Unlike the Han Dynasty (206 B.C.-220 A.D.), more places were making paper, the quantity was bigger and the technology better. Luoyang of Henan, the old papermaking center, saw other centers rising across the country, even in remote areas.

Also, the varieties of paper became more, *Zuobo*, hemp, yellow hemp, cane, and *Yinguang* or "silver light" being famous kinds.

The name of *Zuobo* paper came from its inventor Zuo Bo who lived in present-day Laizhou of Shandong Province. During the Three-Kingdom Period (220-280) this place was called Donglai. On the basis of traditional technology, by borrowing the experience from Cai Lun, he was able to make very neat and very glossy paper perfect for writing. Scholars then rushed for it.

Hemp paper took hemp fiber as the chief material. It is white and water-fast, an ideal material for writing. The famous father and son calligraphers, Wang Xizhi

是当时有名的学者和书法家，他总结历代造纸技艺，借鉴蔡伦造纸的经验，制造出光亮整洁，适于书写用的纸，深受当时文人的欢迎。

麻纸以大麻纤维为主要原料制成，纸质坚韧洁白，耐水浸泡，是理想的书写用纸。东晋著名书法家王羲之、王献之父子常用麻纸练习书法。

黄麻纸是东晋时期在麻纸的基础上研发出的新纸品，也叫"潢纸"。其制作工艺是将麻纸用黄檗汁浸泡，晾干后使用。整个过程被称为"入潢"。经过"入潢"后的黄麻纸，具有防虫蛀蚀的功能。黄麻纸不仅为文人所用，官府文书也常以此纸书写。

藤纸因其主要生产原料为野生藤皮而得名，非常适合书画。这种纸直到唐代仍然为书画家所喜爱。

and Wang Xianzhi during the Eastern Jin Dynasty, used this paper for practice.

Yellow hemp paper was developed from hemp paper, a variety also called *Huangzhi*. It was made with hemp paper being soaked through cork tree water and drying up. This process was called "into the cork tree bark". After this process, paper was insect-proof. This variety was used by scholars and officials alike.

Cane paper got its name from rattan, very good for calligraphic and painting art. Until the Tang Dynasty this variety was still in favor.

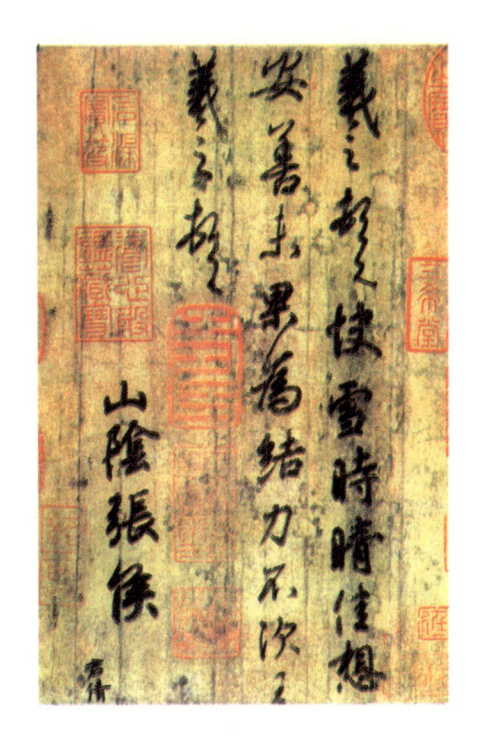

- 藤纸《快雪时晴帖》【局部】
  王羲之（晋）
  Kuaixue Shiqing Tie, or *Calligraphic Work after Snow*, Calligraphic Work on Cane Paper by Wang Xizhi (Jin Dynasty, 265-420)

银光纸产于安徽黟县、歙县一带，纸质光润洁白，采用表面涂布的加工技术，在纸面糊上白色矿物细粉并予以砑光。这种纸的制造，为此后宣纸的出现奠定了工艺基础。

隋唐五代时期的纸

隋唐五代时期，社会文化空前繁荣，文化艺术的兴盛带动了造纸业的发展。

这一时期造纸原料以树皮为主，常见的有楮皮、桑皮，也掺杂其他带有香味的树皮，所制之纸称为"皮纸"。皮纸柔中带劲，纤维交错均匀，易于保存。

此时纸的加工技术在前代的基础之上有很大提高，涂蜡、施胶等新工艺的运用，使纸更加润滑、光洁。其中以硬黄纸较为著名，它是一种较名贵的艺术加工纸，具有莹润的光泽，质地坚韧，透明性强，书写时运笔流利，可久藏，多用于写经和摹写古帖。

除硬黄纸外，这一时期的名贵纸品还有水纹纸、薛涛笺、澄心堂纸等。

Yinguang or the "Silver Light" came from Yixian and Shexian of Anhui Province. This variety features a very white and shiny surface coming from a coating with shiny white mineral particles. The appearance of this paper laid the foundation for the birth of *Xuan* paper in later years.

Paper Made During the Sui, Tang and Five Dynasties

Culture gained a big progress during the Sui, Tang and Five dynasties (581-960) and art activities were booming, which helped the progress of papermaking.

However, the chief materials for papermaking during these periods of history were barks from mulberry and other kinds with fragrance. The paper made with tree bark was called *Pizhi*, meaning it was tough with evenly distributed fiber in it. This variety could be kept for a long time.

The technology was much improved and something new happened like wax coating and glue application to make paper smooth and shiny. The hard yellow paper was the best known, which is tough, shiny, harder and more transparent. It helped uent writing, also,

水纹纸是唐代名纸品，其制造工艺特殊，将纸逐幅在刻有字画的文版上碾磨，或用刻有纹理、图案的模子置于纸面进行碾磨，纸面上便隐起各种花纹图案，放在迎光处可显现透亮的线纹图案。此种纸多用作信纸、诗笺、书法帖纸。

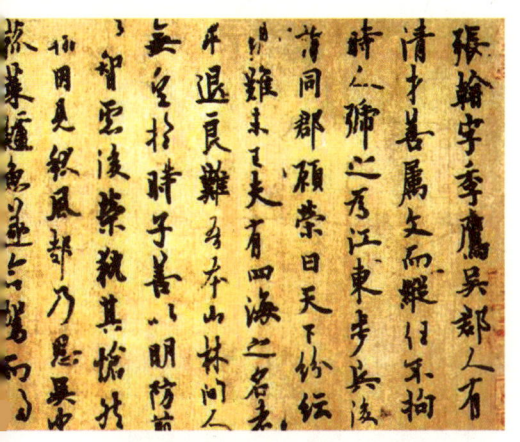

- 水纹纸《张翰帖》【局部】欧阳询（唐）
Zhang Han Tie, (Partial) Calligraphic Work on Water Wave Paper by Ouyang Xun (Tang Dynasty, 618-907)

薛涛笺是唐末五代名笺纸，因由女诗人薛涛创制而得名。薛涛笺是一种加工染色纸，属于红色小幅诗笺，其特点是省料、加工方便、生产成本低。

could be kept longer than other kinds. This variety was often used for Buddhist sutra writing or copying of ancient calligraphy works.

Other famous varieties during these periods were water waves, *Xuetao*, *Chengxintang* and so on, named after their inventor, a famous literary man or their birthplace.

Water Wave was a famous kind during the Tang Dynasty. It came from a very special making process: carving the pattern or characters onto a plate, rubbing this paper against the plate until the paper picking up the patterns or characters. Against light this paper showed a beautiful pattern on the surface. It was a very romantic material for letters, poetry writing or calligraphic works.

Xuetao paper, a dyed paper popular in the late Tang (618-907) and Five dynasties (907-960) that followed got its name from the famous female poet Xue Tao. It was often red and in a small size for writing an improvised poem, a paper of less cost and easy to make.

笺纸

笺纸又称"花笺""诗笺""彩笺""尺牍",是供人写信作诗用的小张书画纸,产生于南北朝时期,当时称"八行笺"。从唐宋开始一直到明清,笺纸十分流行,比较有名的有薛涛笺、谢公笺等。

另外,还有一种印有诗文图画的信笺,属于工艺用纸,叫作"笺谱"。最具代表性的名笺谱是明代的《十竹斋笺谱》《萝轩变古笺谱》。笺谱由于所绘图画大都出于名家之手而具有较高的收藏价值和艺术价值。

• 笺纸 金冬心手札(清)
Jin Dongxin's Calligraphy on Letter Paper (Qing Dynasty, 1616-1911)

Letter Paper

This variety had other names, flower paper, poetry paper, color paper ... It was for the writing of a small size calligraphic work or painting, or writing a letter or a poem. The first time it appeared was in the Southern and Northern dynasties under the name of "eight line paper". It was popular during the Tang and Song dynasties and down to the Ming and Qing dynasties. Famous styles in this variety were *Xuetao* and *Xiegong* papers.

Jianpu was a kind with printed poems or paintings on it. The most representative form of this kind was the Ming-dynasty *Shizhu Zhai* and *Luoxuan Biangu*. The paintings they carried were often the prints of works by renowned artists. Because of this, this variety was highly collectable and artistically valuable.

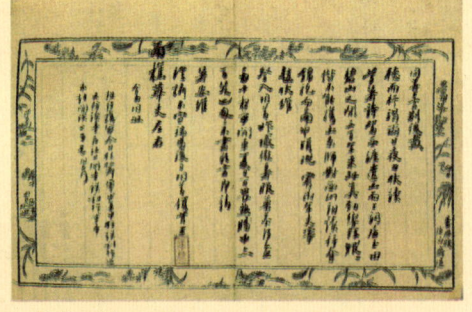

• 笺谱(清)
Jianpu Paper (Qing Dynasty, 1616-1911)

澄心堂纸是徽州地区所产的一种宣纸，是南唐后主李煜命人专为宫廷所制。此纸以楮树皮为主要原料，纸质柔韧细腻，光滑吸墨，因李煜将此纸藏于自己读书批奏章的处所澄心堂内而得名。后世视澄心堂纸为艺术珍品，存世者极为稀少。

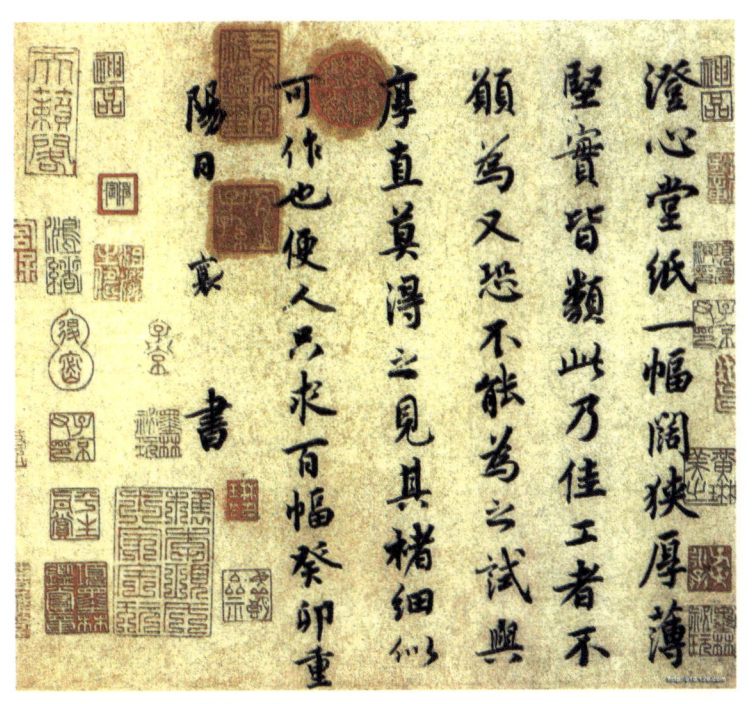

Chengxintang was a *Xuan* paper from Huizhou, said to have been made for royal use only by the instruction of Li Yu, ruler of the Southern Tang of the Ten States. This variety has a very fine texture, glossy and is very good at absorbing ink. Because Li Yu kept it inside his study *Chengxin Tang*, it got its name. To later generations, this paper was priceless, very little to have come down in history.

- 《澄心堂纸帖》 蔡襄（宋）
Chengxintang Zhi Tie, by Cai Xiang (Song Dynasty, 960-1279)

梅尧臣得纸赋诗

梅尧臣（1002—1060），北宋著名的现实主义诗人。他每次得到佳纸必赋诗，以此表达心中的激动欣喜。一次，梅尧臣的挚友欧阳修得到十张宫内的澄心堂纸，赠予梅尧臣数张"佳物共享"。梅尧臣得纸后，激动不已，写下《永叔寄澄心堂纸二幅》。

Poem Composed by Mei Yaochen after He Received *Cheng Xin Tang* paper

Mei Yaochen (1002-1060), a poet of realism school during the Northern Song Dynasty (1127-1279), was said to compose a poem each time he received a rare variety of paper. Once after he received a couple of sheets of *Chengxintang* paper as a gift from his close friend Ouyang Xiu, who had received ten from somewhere, Mei Yaochen was so excited that he wrote a famous poem titled "*Upon the Receipt of Two Sheets of Chengxintang Paper*".

• 梅尧臣像
Mei Yaochen

宣纸

宣纸是中国古代造纸业中重要的纸类，它从唐代开始便是中国社会的主流用纸，在文化传承中起了重要的作用。

宣纸因产于宣州而得名，其原料有檀树皮、楮树皮、桑树皮、竹、麻等数十种。相传宣纸是蔡伦的后世弟子孔丹在晋代创制。一次，孔丹在河边发现了一棵老檀树倒在河水里。经过河水浸泡，檀树皮的纤维被漂白，孔丹取其纤维制纸，宣纸由此而成。

宣纸洁白如玉、绵韧而坚、柔软均匀。这种纸利于书画创作，润墨性强，墨晕层次分明。另外它还有耐老化、防虫蛀、耐热、耐光的性能，适合长期保存，有"千年美纸""纸中之王"的美称。宣纸被大量运用于书画领域，而且被推广到木版水印、装潢裱托、拓片印刷及贵重档案资料保存等方面。

宣纸按加工方法的不同，可分为生宣、熟宣、半熟宣三种。生宣是没有经过额外加工的宣纸，吸水性和沁水性都强，水墨渗沁迅速，易产生丰富的墨韵变化，多用于绘制泼墨画和写意山水画。熟宣是宣纸加工时涂以明矾，纸质比生宣硬，吸水能力弱，使用时墨和颜料不会洇散开来，但久藏会出现漏矾和脆裂的现象，多用于绘制工笔画和书写楷书、隶书。半熟宣是用生宣浸以各种植物汁液而成，具有微弱的抗水力。其特点是较熟宣易吸水，又不似生宣那样容易化水，主要适

- **宣纸（现代）**
  Xuan Paper (Modern Times)

- **《五牛图》韩滉（唐）**
  宣纸适合长期保存，这幅《五牛图》历经千余年仍然保持着原画的风貌。
  Five Oxen, by Han Huang (Tang Dynasty, 618-907)
  Xuan paper is almost ageless. This painting, after more than a thousand years, is still in good shape.

用于书写小幅屏条、册页或用作兼工带写的绘画。

另外，宣纸按用料不同，又可分为棉料、净皮、特净三类。棉料是指原材料檀皮含量在40%左右的纸，较薄、较轻；净皮是指檀皮含量达到60%以上的纸；而特净是原材料檀皮的含量达到80%以上的纸。皮料成分越重，纸张越能经受拉力，质量也越好，更能体现丰富的墨迹层次和润墨效果，越能经受笔力，并且反复搓揉而纸面不会破。

每种宣纸又有单宣、夹宣、二层、三层之分，规格上有四尺、六尺、八尺、丈二、丈四、丈八等区别。

- 半熟宣书法（清）
Calligraphy on "the Medium" *Xuan* Paper (Qing Dynasty, 1616-1911)

Xuan Paper

An important kind of paper made in ancient China, ever since its birth the *Xuan* paper has been the chief means for writing in society, and was very important to the progress of Chinese culture.

It got its name from its birthplace Xuanzhou. Among its materials were barks from wingceltis, mulberry, bamboo and hemp … This variety was said invented by a follower of Cai Lun named Kong Dan during the Jin Dynasty (265-420). Once, he saw a wingceltis tree soaked in river water which had bleached its fibers. He tried to make paper with these fibers so the *Xuan* paper was born.

Xuan paper was white, tough and soft, very good for painting and calligraphic writing. It absorbed more ink than any other kind and was able to give a dream-like feeling. It withstood

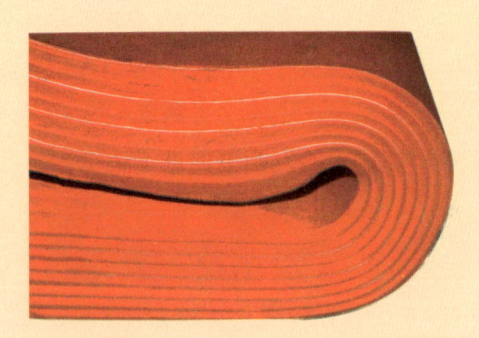

- 宣纸（现代）
Xuan Paper (Modern Times)

aging and threats from insects, heat and light. It could be kept for a long time and because of this it was named "paper of thousand years" and "king of papers". It was seen in many art forms like woodblock printing, mounting, rubbing, and recording of important documents.

By different processing *Xuan* paper can be classified as *Shengxuan* or "raw *Xuan*", *Shuxuan* or "cooked *Xuan*" and *Banshuxuan* "the medium". *Shengxuan* was *Xuan* paper without additional processing but very hydrophilic; ink applied to it spread quickly to produce a cloud-like look. This type was good for ink-splashing landscape. *Shuxuan* had alums added, crispy and less hydrophilic, difficult for ink to spread on. Long storage might have alums leak and paper breaks. This variety was good for *Gongbi* style painting, official scripts and regular scripts. *Banshuxuan* came with *Shengxuan* paper processed with juice extract from plants. It was less hydrophilic, something between Shu and Sheng kinds. This kind was good for writing small-size hanging scrolls and painting albums with calligraphy to go with.

Xuan paper can also be classified into three types by materials: the cotton, the pure and the purist. The cotton referred to *Xuan* paper with 40 percent of wingceltis bark fiber, often thinner and lighter. The pure referred to 60 percent of wingceltis bark fiber, while the purist, above 80 percent. The more wingceltis fiber it contained the more endurable, tougher and of better quality the paper was, able to show different shades of ink and to withstand rough handling.

Xuan paper has a single layer, the lined, two layers, and even three layers types. It had different sizes from 4 *chi* per side to 6, 8, 12, 14 even 18 *chi* per side.

宋元时期的纸

宋元时期，造纸术得到进一步发展，印刷术的发明更促进了造纸产业的扩张。

宋元制纸原料就地取材，沿用树皮的同时，还引入竹、麦秆等材料。在盛产竹子的南方制造出洁白柔软、浸润保墨、纤维细腻、绵韧平整的竹纸，深得文人墨客的青睐。

Paper Made During the Song and Yuan Dynasties

Papermaking further progressed during the Song and Yuan dynasties (960-1368), particularly after the invention of printing.

Papermaking during the Song and Yuan dynasties took local materials and apart from tree barks, included bamboo and wheat stalks. In the south, where

宋代制纸业将前代的砑光、染色等技术加以发挥，发明了金粟笺纸、谢公笺、元书纸、明仁殿纸等名纸。

金粟笺纸是一种盛产于歙州的以桑皮为原料的纸，因浙江海盐金粟山下的金粟寺用其大量抄写经书而得名。其特点是质地硬密，表面光滑，纤维分布均匀，呈半透明，一面呈浅黄色，一面呈深黄色，防蛀抗水，寿命很长，虽历千年，犹如新制。

谢公笺是一种经过染色加工的纸，为文人谢景初所创，因色彩丰富又名"十色笺"，也就是十种颜色的书写专用纸。这种纸色彩艳丽新颖，雅致有趣，有深红、粉红、杏红、明黄、深青、浅青、深绿、浅绿、铜绿、浅云十种色，在历史上与唐代的薛涛笺齐名。

元书纸是一种采用当年生的嫩毛竹作为原料，以手工抄造制成的书写用纸，在北宋真宗时期（998—1022）被选作御用文书纸，因皇帝元祭（元日庙祭）时用以书写祭文而称"元书纸"。其特点是洁白柔韧，微含竹子清香，落水易溶，着

bamboo was abundant, very white and very soft bamboo paper was made, good in absorbing ink with a finer texture. This paper was much welcomed by scholars and artists.

Song-dynasty papermaking took coloring a step further. It invented new kinds, many being famous in history.

Jinsu was made with mulberry bark in Shezhou. It got its name from a temple in Zhejiang, which requested a large quantity of *Xuan* paper for copying sutras. This *Jinsu* paper had a strong and closely knitted texture, very fine and smooth with evenly distributed fiber, transparent to some degree, yellowish on one side and dark yellow on the other, mothproof and waterproof. It had a long life span, even after a thousand years it might still look as good as new.

Xiegong paper was colored, which got its name from famous scholar Xie Jingchu. Because of bright colors it had it was also called "ten-color paper", which meant "writing paper in ten different colors", equally famous as *Xuetao* paper during the Tang.

The *Yuanshu* writing paper took fresh bamboo as its material. During the Emperor Zhenzong' reign (998-1022) of the Northern Song Dynasty

墨不渗，久藏不蛀、不变色。

明仁殿纸是元代的一种加工纸，专供宫廷内府使用。明仁殿是皇帝看书的地方，这种纸供皇帝御用，所以叫"明仁殿纸"。由于此纸名贵，在明清时期多有仿制。

宋元时期纸的幅制也有改进，可制造远大于前代的巨幅纸。这是宋代制纸技术进步的重要标志。南宋时期，还开创了对纸的再利用技

it was selected as paper for royal use, especially for writing memorial articles to be read in a memorializing ceremony for the bygone emperors. It featured a white color and a very pleasant smell; it easily dissolved in water but difficult for ink to ooze, also mothproof and its color lasting longer.

The *Mingrendian* paper during the Yuan Dynasty (1206-1368) was for royal use only. It got its name from the palace where emperors read and wrote. Because of its tremendous fame its imitations were made in later dynasties of the Ming and Qing dynasties.

Changes also happened to the size. During the Song and Yuan dynasties a much bigger format than before was made and this marked a big progress. Recycling of used paper began during the Southern Song, which processed the used paper into new ones. The recycled paper had an interesting name, "back to life" paper. Recycled paper marked the maturity of papermaking technology.

Monographs of papermaking technology appeared during the Song Dynasty, as was seen in the "Introductions to Paper", a chapter in *The Four Treasures of the Study* authored by Su Yijian. This chapter was probably the

术，将使用过的纸作为原料，进行制作、加工成为新纸，名为"还魂纸"。这种再造纸是技术成熟的重要表现。

宋代还出现了关于纸的专著——苏易简所著《文房四谱》中的《纸谱》，这是中国最早的制纸专著。宋代雕版印刷术的发展，不但促进了印书业的发展，还带动了制纸业的发展。

earliest writing about papermaking. Also in the Song Dynasty, lithography came into being, which boosted book printing as well as papermaking.

纸与印刷术

中国印刷术是人类文明史上具有划时代意义的发明。它是在笔、墨、纸都具备的物质条件下才创造出来的，其中纸在印刷过程中的作用是无可替代的，是关键的材料。

在印刷之前，需要在纸上先誊写样本，经过校对、上板、刻版等工序，做成上有凸

- 毛边纸、毛太纸
Bamboo Paper with Rough Edges Called *Maobian* or *Maotai*.

起文字的雕版，然后涂以墨汁，以白纸铺在雕版上，经过擦刷后取下晾平，即成一页。这就是原始的印刷术，印刷用纸多选用纸面光滑、纸质均匀、吸墨适量的竹制毛边纸和毛太纸。

Paper and Printing

Printing was an epoch-making invention in the history of civilization, coming only after the writing brush, ink and paper had appeared. The most important catalyst for the birth of printing was paper, whose role couldn't be overestimated.

  Before printing began, a copy was made on paper first, then, after proofreading, transferred by carving onto plates as embossment. After ink was applied on the plate, blank paper was spread onto the place to apply repeated brushing until it picked up the characters. Then, it was sent for drying and this was the primitive form of printing. The paper used was often made from bamboo with rough edges but glossy with fine texture and right degree of ink absorption.

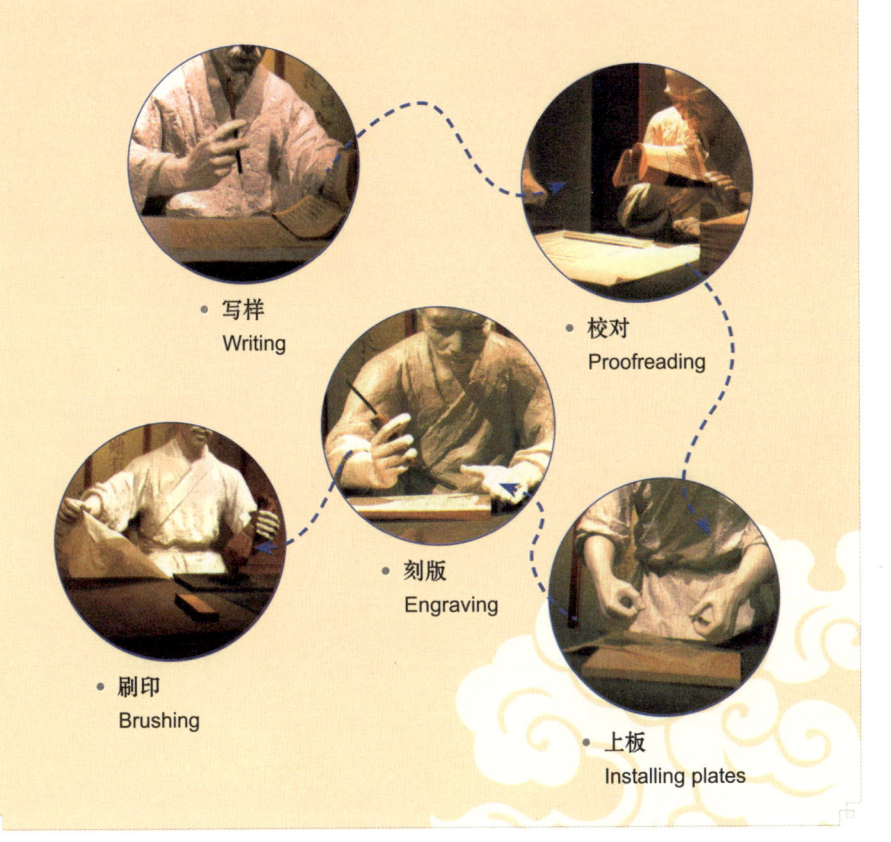

• 写样 Writing

• 校对 Proofreading

• 刻版 Engraving

• 刷印 Brushing

• 上板 Installing plates

明清时期的纸

明清时期，造纸工艺进一步发展，造纸原料及生产技术都有了很大的突破，出现了许多精品，特别是一些精美的纸笺不仅仅是书画用纸，其本身就是一件赏心悦目的艺术品。如羊脑笺、贡笺、砑花纸、五色粉蜡笺等。

羊脑笺是明代的一种名贵纸，这种纸以存放较久的羊脑和顶烟墨涂于纸上，再经砑光工序制成。其特点是黑如漆、明如镜，用泥金写经，可防虫蛀，历久不坏。

贡笺是明代名纸，制于明宣德年间，是一种加工纸，其制作技艺十分精湛。这种纸有许多品种，如本色纸、五色粉笺、金花五色笺、五色大帘纸、磁青纸等，其颜色是经专门的染料浸染而来的。

砑花纸是明清以来一种新的加工纸。纸料为上等较坚韧的皮纸，有厚有薄，图案多为山水、花鸟、鱼虫、龙凤、云纹或水纹，也有人物故事或文字。纸的表面施粉，非常精细，很适于笔墨书写。

五色粉蜡笺也是一种加工纸，始于唐代，盛行于清代。这种纸为

Paper Made During the Ming and Qing Dynasties

During the Ming Dynasty (1368-1644) and the Qing Dynasty (1616-1911), progress was made in both material and making technology. Famous varieties appeared. Some of them, no longer made for painting and calligraphy, were works of art. These varieties included *Yangnao*, *Gongjian*, *Yahua* and Five-color Pink Wax.

Yangnao was a very famous and expensive kind made during the Ming Dynasty, made by applying lamb brains and top-class soot ink to surface. It is exceptionally black and glossy, perfect for sutra writing in gold characters and able to withstand damage from insects.

Gongjian was a famous processed variety that first appeared during the Xuande Period of the Ming Dynasty. It had varieties, the original color, five-color, golden, five-color big and *Ciqing*. Their colors came by soaking in special pigments.

Yahua paper, a new variety, was born during the Ming and Qing dynasties, made from tough paper of different thickness. It often had patterns like landscape, flower and bird, fish and insects, loong and

多层黏合纸，底料的皮纸施以粉并加染蓝、白、粉红、淡绿、黄等五色，加蜡以手工捶轧砑光制成，故称"五色粉蜡笺"。这种纸的特点是防水性强，表面光滑，透明度好，防虫蛀，可以长久存放。

- 竹纹砑花纸 书札（明）
Letter on *Yahua* Paper with Bamboo Lines (Ming Dynasty, 1368-1644)

明清时期还兴起了仿制纸的热潮。明代仿制了唐代的"薛涛笺"和宋代的"金粟山藏经纸"。这种仿制纸在制作时加入了云母粉，纸面显出光亮耀眼的颗粒，是明代人的创新。清代时仿制的纸品种更多，尤其是康熙、乾隆年间的仿制

phoenix, cloud and water waves, human figures, even written characters. Very fine powder was applied onto surface, very good for writing with brushes.

Wuse or Five-color Pink Wax Paper came from the Tang Dynasty but reached its peak during the Qing Dynasty. This paper had multiple layers on a tough paper foundation, often dyed blue, white, pink, pale green or yellow. After being waxed by hand, it was done. This paper was waterproof and mothproof, glossy and transparent, able to last for a long time.

A passion for making imitations of ancient varieties happened during the Ming and Qing dynasties. The Ming Dynasty had imitations of *Xuetao* paper from the Tang Dynasty and the *Jinsu* paper from the Song Dynasty. With mica powder added to their pulp, these imitations shimmered against light. This was a Ming invention. Imitations made during the Qing Dynasty became even more prevalent, particularly

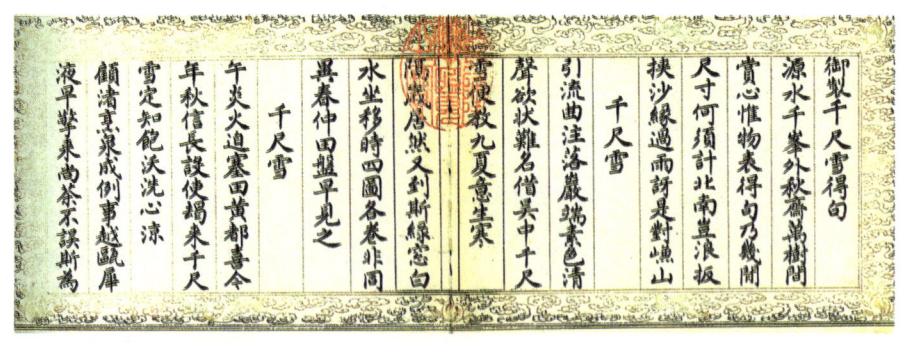

• 蜡笺《御制千尺雪得句》（清）
Wang Youdun's Writing after Snow, Bearing Emperor Qianlong's Seal Stamp for Book Collection, on Wax Paper(Qing Dynasty, 1616-1911)

纸品最为精细，不仅保留了原纸的特点，还用泥金绘制各种精美图案作为装饰，并且清楚标注仿制的时间和品名，供内府收藏和保管。

during the Kangxi and Qianlong periods. Not only preserving original features, the imitations had something new to it, say, a decoration painted in gold. They also bore the name of the variety they were after and the time they were made. Usually, they were collected by the interior office of the Forbidden City.

纸的制作流程
Steps of Papermaking

纸的制作要经过以下步骤。

Papermaking had the following steps.

❶ ❷

取坯：造纸的第一道工序，是将藤、竹、麻、树皮等原料搜集起来，然后将选好的原料结成捆进行蒸煮、脱皮，最后再将这些毛料浸泡在石灰水里，若干天后取出洗净，这就是制纸的坯料。

Material collection: this was the first step, which meant select cane, bamboo, hemp and tree bark, and bundle them for steaming, boiling and debarking before they were placed in lime water for a couple of days. Then, they were washed clean. By now, the materials were ready.

制料：造纸的重要一步，对皮坯进行反复的浸渍、蒸煮、洗涤和暴晒，其目的是去除杂质，提纯纤维。

Materials processing: a crucial step, which meant repeated soaking, steaming, boiling, washing and drying in the sun. This step was to remove impurities to get clean fibers.

③

④

打浆：将经过制料的坯料浸在草木灰水中，历时十多天后即可发酵为浆料。然后把浆料放入臼中，舂成纸浆。

Pulp making: leave the processed materials in lime water for a dozen of days before they were fermented and pounded into pulp in a mortar.

抄纸（捞纸）：把纸浆倒进石槽里，加胶或者纸药水以及木槿汁，使之具有黏性，然后持竹帘进入水槽，将纸浆抄进帘内以滤去水分并形成纸胎，再将纸胎平放在湿纸板上。

Chaozhi or paper lifting: pulp in mortar received glue, medicine and hibiscus juice to make it sticky. Then, lowered a bamboo sieve into the pulp and lifted it with a layer of pulp on it. After water was drained away the layer became the rough form of paper to be placed on a wet board.

⑤ 焙纸：等平放在湿纸板上的纸胎叠够一定的张数后，将其压干，然后再把纸一张张揭开，贴到光洁的砖砌的夹墙上。夹墙里烧着柴火，用炙热的墙面把纸烘干。这样，一张手工纸就初步制成了。

Baking: when layers reached the right number they were pressed to release water. Then peel them off sheet by sheet, and paste them on a wall with fire inside. The heat will completely dry the paper. By now, a sheep of hand-made paper was done.

加工纸则是在以上步骤完成之后再进行加工制作而成，常见的加工方法有以下几种。

Additional processing was given for special needs. Common additional processing was the following.

砑光：用光滑的卵石在纸面上来回压磨，使纸面光滑。这项工艺在东汉末年就已出现。

Calendaring: rub very smooth pebbles on paper until the paper became very smooth. This processing first appeared in the late Eastern Han Dynasty.

染色：用有机染料给纸染色，最初染黄色者居多，后来各种色彩的纸纷纷涌现。

Coloring: dye with organic pigments into yellow at the beginning, more colors appeared later.

施粉：在纸有孔隙的地方用粉加以填补。最初的目的是填补孔隙，后来将它与彩色一起混合，用来调和色彩，色彩斑斓的粉纸由此产生。

Powder application: the original purpose was to fill up tiny apertures on paper. Later, pigments were added to powder for a colorful look.

洒金：洒金的目的是使纸面看上去更加绚丽夺目，富丽华贵，通常是在彩色的粉纸上撒上金银粉末。在洒金之前，要在纸面上涂上黏合剂，撒上金银粉末后再进行砑光。

- 施过粉的小笺（清）
Paper after Receiving Powder (Qing Dynasty, 1616-1911)

Scattering gold powder: this was to give the paper a very luxurious look by applying gold or silver powder. The paper received a coat of adhesive first and calendaring after powder was applied.

印花：印花有两种方法，一种是印明花，直接将图案印在纸面上；一种是印暗花，是在抄纸过程中将纸压在两块一正一反刻有凸凹花纹图案的木刻版中间，逐幅印制。

- 洒金云龙纹色绢纸（清）
Color Paper Having Received Gold Powder, Printed with a Cloud and Loong Pattern (Qing Dynasty, 1616-1911)

Stamping: there were two ways: one was to print a pattern directly on paper and the other was to squeeze together two patterned wood plates, one in intaglio, the other in relief.

> 纸的种类

纸的种类主要是根据不同的造纸原料来划分的，古代用于造纸的原料主要有麻、树皮、藤、竹、草等，因此纸可分为麻纸、皮纸、藤纸、竹纸、草纸等。

麻纸是以麻为主要原料制成的纸。从造纸术诞生到东晋时期，麻纸一直是主流用纸。蔡伦造纸所用的原料是破渔网、破布等麻类纤维，所造之纸也属于麻纸。

> Varieties of Paper

By materials, paper can be classified into different types. Because ancient times used hemp, tree bark, cane, bamboo and weed, paper made from them picked up similar names, hemp paper, bast paper, cane paper, bamboo paper and weed paper.

Hemp paper took hemp as its material. Ever since the birth of papermaking to the East Jin Dynasty hemp was its major material. The old fishing nets and rags Cai Lun used for papermaking contained hemp fibers, therefore such paper was called hemp paper.

- 麻
  Hemp

皮纸是以各种树皮制成的纸，包括桑树皮、楮树皮、青檀树皮、木芙蓉树皮等。皮纸纤维长，纸质洁白细嫩，柔韧性好，张力强，吸水性和透气性好，光滑度高，有清香味，不易变色，保存年代久，是古人书写重要契约及经文的首选纸。

● 树皮
Tree bark

藤纸是以藤皮所制的纸，最出名的藤纸是剡藤纸，因产于剡县(今浙江省嵊州市)而得名。其特点是薄、轻、韧、细、白，莹润光泽，坚滑而不凝笔，质地优良。

竹纸主要以嫩竹制成，产生于唐代，宋代以后便被普遍推广开来，其产地在江浙一带。竹纸成本低廉，书写流畅，纸面光洁，吸湿性强，纸张整洁、干燥，质薄无碎屑，色泽均匀，无异味。

Bast paper took barks from mulberry, wingceltis and hibiscus as material. Bast paper had long fiber, very white and smooth in appearance and supple. It was highly expansive, hydrophilic, gauzy, smooth and fragrant. Bast paper could be kept for a long time without losing its color. Bast paper was often used for copying sutras and important documents.

Cane paper, as its name suggests, came from the skin of cane. The most famous in this variety came from Shanxian County (today's Shengzhou of Zhejiang). Cane paper was thin, light, tough, fine, white and glossy, easy for brush tips to move upon.

Bamboo paper was made from tender

● 藤
Cane

• 竹
Bamboo

草纸是以植物茎类制造的纸，比较粗糙，易出墨晕，不适宜书写。

bamboo, an invention made during the Tang Dynasty, becoming popular in the Song Dynasty. The biggest production places of this variety were Jiangsu and Zhejiang. Low cost, easy to be written upon, smooth on surface, neat in format, dry, thin and less breakable, evenly colored and having no funny odor, these were the characteristics of this kind.

Weed paper came from plant stems. This variety had its disadvantages: rough in texture, easy for ink to ooze and not very good for writing.

纸的装订

在中国古代，纸的装订形式经历了一个演变的过程。从最初沿袭帛书的卷轴装，再向册页发展，衍生出经折装、旋风装等多种形式。五代时出现了蝴蝶装，后来又改用包背装，最后是线装。

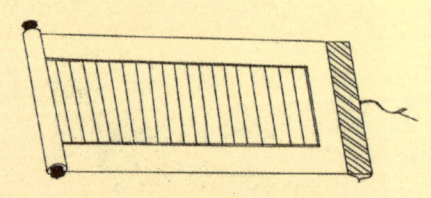

• **卷轴装**
最早的装订方式，阅读时可逐渐展开，阅毕卷起即可。这种装帧形式至今仍用于书画的装裱。

Roll Binding
Roll binding was the earliest form with the advantage of easy unrolling for reading and rolling after reading was done. This form is still used for the mounting of paintings or calligraphic works.

Paper Binding

Paper binding experienced a long time of progress, from silk book scroll at the beginning to albumed pages, it had many forms before it reached thread binding. One form of this variety named "the butterfly" appeared during the Five dynasties, followed by *Baobei* and finally the thread binding.

- 经折装

将一幅长卷沿着文字版面的间隔中缝，一反一正地折叠起来，形成长方形的一叠，阅读起来比卷轴装方便许多。

Sutra Binding
This was to fold a long sheet of paper along the central straight line and reverse alternatively to make a rectangular book. This form was easier to read than the roll binding.

- 旋风装

在经折装的基础上，将一张纸对折后一半粘在第一页，一半粘在最后一页，避免散页的问题。

Xuanfeng Binding
This was, after sutra binding, folding the paper to reduce its size by half, pasting one end of the folded paper to the first page and the other end to the last page. This binding had no loose page problem.

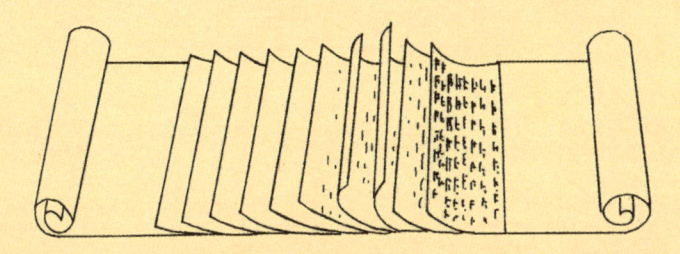

- 龙鳞装

又称"鱼鳞装"，是将散页依次序像鱼鳞一样粘在一张卷轴式的纸上。

Longlin Binding
Also named *Yulin* binding, this binding was to paste loose pages onto a paper roll like fish scales.

- 蝴蝶装

起源于唐代，流行于宋代的装订形式，由于版面犹如蝴蝶展翅而得名。将有文字的两页对折，将折叠处粘连在硬纸上，翻阅时会出现无字的背面。

Butterfly Binding

First seen during the Tang Dynasty, becoming popular during the Song Dynasty, this variety got its name from its resemblance to a butterfly. This was to fold two pages with printed sides into folio and paste it onto board paper. When being leafed, unprinted side was shown.

- 包背装

书页背对背地折叠起来，将书页的两边粘在书脊上。避免了蝴蝶装阅读时出现白页的问题。

Baobei Binding

Each page was folded back to back before being pasted onto the book spine. This binding had no blank page as seen in the butterfly binding.

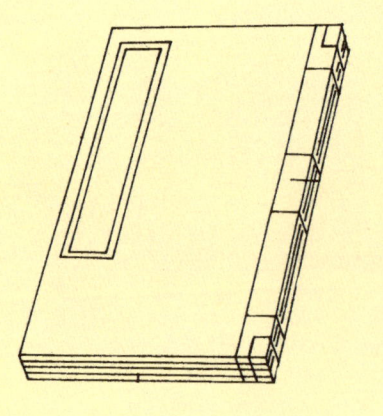

- 线装

用两张半页纸，分置于书页的前后，与书册一起装订，避免了包背装书背处容易破损的问题。

Thread Binding

Two sheets of soft paper are bounded together with the book, one at the beginning of the book and the other at its end to make the spine stronger.

具有收藏价值的古籍
Collectable Ancient Books

　　古籍是古纸做成的,很多古纸都是以古籍的形式流传保留至今的。具有收藏价值的古籍有以下几种。

Ancient books had ancient paper in them and much ancient paper that came down in history is seen in this form. The most collectable ancient books are the following.

符合"三性九类"的古籍

　　"三性"是指具有三种特性的古籍:因古籍年代久远而具有的"历史文物性";因古籍内容有重要参考价值而具有的"学术资料性";因古籍的雕版印制考究、插图精美等而具有的"艺术代表性"。

　　"九类"是指九种古籍:一是元代或元代以前刻印或抄写的书本;二是明代刻印或抄写的书本(版本模糊、流传较多的除外);三是清代乾隆及乾隆以前流传较少的刻本、抄本;四是太平天国及历代农民革命政权所印行的书本;五是辛亥革命前,在学术研究上有独到见解或有学派特点以及流传很少的刻本、抄本;六是辛亥革命前反映某一时期、某一领域或某一事件资料方面的稿本及较少见的刻本、抄本;七是辛亥革命前有名人、学者批校、题跋,或抄录前人批校而有参考价值的刻本、抄本;八是在印刷上能反映中国印刷技术发展、代表一定时期印刷水平的各种活字本、套印本,或有较精版画的刻本;九是明代印谱、清代集古印谱、名家篆刻的钤印本、有特色或有亲笔题记的书本。

Ancient Books of Three Unique Significance in Nine Categories

Three unique significances mean "historical significance", because of such books being printed centuries ago; "academic significance", because of the information they give; "artistic significance" from exquisite engraving and illustrations.

　　The nine categories are as follows: printed or hand-written in or before the Yuan Dynasty(1206-1368); printed or hand-written in the Ming Dynasty(1368-1644) or prior to the Ming Dynasty (not including less clear editions or the edition with many copies in circulation); printed or hand-written with few copies in circulation during and before the Qianlong Period (1736-1795) of the Qing Dynasty; books issued by farmers regimes like the "Taiping Heavenly Kingdom" (1851-1864); academically valuable books of rare editions; books and records about a certain period of time, a certain event in history or a field either printed or hand-written prior to the 1911 Revolution; printed or hand-written editions with inscriptions of or annotated by famous personage; books that may show the progress of Chinese printing technology, printed with movable types or chromatograph edition or with highly artistic illustrations; collections of stamp prints or inscriptions or carvings from famous personage of the Ming and Qing dynasties.

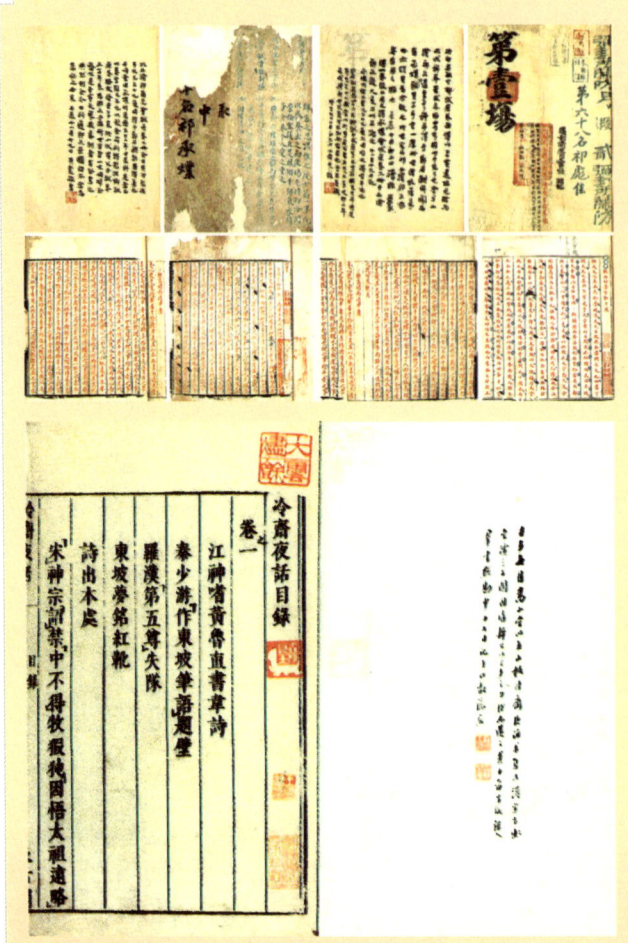

- 试卷（明）
  Test Paper (Ming Dynasty, 1368-1644)

- 王国维手校线装本《冷斋夜话》（清）
  Lengzhai Yehua or Idle Talks in Cold Study at Night, a Thread Bound Edition Annotated by Wang Guowei (Qing Dynasty, 1616-1911)

特殊版本的古籍

古籍的版本是决定其收藏价值的重要因素。通常，木刻本价值高于石印本；石印本价值高于铅印本。此外，初版的古籍价值要高于再版和重复印刷的。

Special Ancient Editions

Edition determines the value of book collection. Usually, block printed edition is more valuable than a lithography edition and a lithography edition is more valuable than a stereotype edition. The first edition and the first print are more valuable than later editions and later prints.

纸张轻盈的古籍

纸张的轻盈程度也是决定古籍价值高低的一个因素，古籍纸张越轻，用纸越高档，收藏价值越高。

Ancient Books Printed on Paper of Light Weight

Weight of paper also determines the value of an ancient book. The lighter the paper, which means better quality, the more valuable the book is.

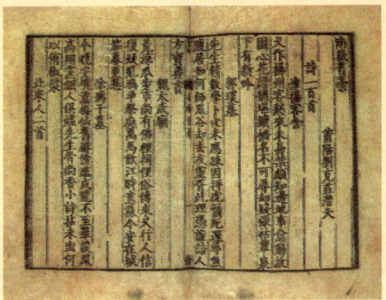

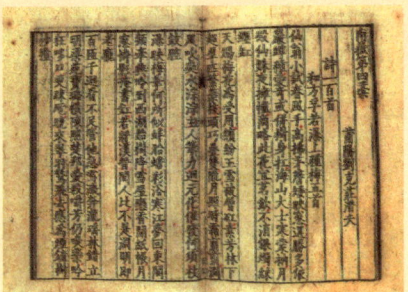

- 《南岳旧稿》（宋）

Nanyue Jiugao (Song Dynasty, 960-1279)

题材独特的古籍

题材内容越独特的古籍具有越高的收藏价值。一般来说，在经史子集里，子集类古籍的收藏价值相对较高。明清以后的古籍，则以那些记载了重大历史事件的工具书，传记书，记录特殊年代、特殊事件的古籍最有收藏价值。

Ancient Books with Unique Subject Matter

The more unique the subject matter, the more valuable the book is. Among all the books of classical studies, philosophy and literature books have a bigger value, so are the books after the Ming and Qing dynasties of significant events, biography or chronicles.

发行量少的古籍

"物以稀为贵"是收藏的一大准则。很多古籍之所以价格高昂，就是因为各种原因导致能较完整流传下来的很少。

Editions with Little Print Run

When a thing becomes rare, it is precious — this is a common saying among collectors. The high value of ancient books is determined by their small number of complete ones that have come down to the present day.

古纸的保存

古纸的保存要注意防潮、防虫、防晒、防干裂、防烟熏和油污、防折叠等。

防潮：久藏的古纸一旦受潮，就会出现水渍和霉点。防止古纸受潮的办法是在纸的外面用一层皮纸包裹，然后放于盒中，置于干燥、凉爽、通风之处。

防虫：虫会咬噬古纸，造成古纸破损，可在存纸的地方放置一些驱避剂，如麝香、芸草等。

防晒：古纸经过强烈的阳光照射后很容易裂开，纸色也会变黄，所以应尽量避免阳光、灯光的直射。

防烟熏和油污：古纸不应长期放在有烟气熏染的地方，在检视古纸时切忌手上有油污。另外，尽量不要用手直接抚摸纸。

防折叠：古纸应尽量用卷的方式来收藏，折叠容易破坏其品相。

Keeping of Ancient Paper

The keeping of ancient paper must be damp free, mothproof, out of sunshine, away from smoke, oil and folding threats and seasoning crack free.

Moisture-proof: affected by damp mildew and water, marks appear. Prevention against this is to wrap ancient paper with a sheet of bast paper before leaving it in a box, to be placed in a dry, shady and ventilated place.

Mothproof: insects make a big threat to the paper and insect repellents like musk or cloud weed should be left next to the paperwork.

Out of sunshine: direct sunshine makes ancient paper crack and turn yellow so ancient paper should never be left in sunshine or exposed to lamplight.

Keep the paper off oil and smoke. Ancient paper should be kept off either smoke or oil, even the oil on hand. Direct contact should be avoided.

Ancient paper should be rolled for keeping. Folding seriously damages its looks.

- 宣统御制宣纸（清）
  The *Xuan* Paper Made During the Xuantong Period for Royal Use only (Qing Dynasty, 1616-1911)

砚
Inkstone

砚，是研墨的工具，同笔、墨、纸一起共同记录着中国古老的历史和悠久的文化。砚的材质和式样丰富多彩，是文房四宝中流传至今数量最多的。砚的制作融合了中国传统雕刻、绘画、文学等因素，凝结了众多制砚匠人的智慧。

Like the writing brush, ink sticks and paper, the inkstone in different fashions and materials has recorded Chinese history and culture. Of the four treasures of the study, ancient inkstones that have survived history are more in numbers than the rest three. Their making shows the values of traditional Chinese sculpture, painting and literature. It was a product of collective wisdom from craftsmen.

> 砚的历史

砚的历史悠久，最初与研磨棒一起配套使用。砚的材质很多，但除了石砚、瓷砚、玉砚外，其他材质的古砚目前已很少见到完整之物。

砚的发端

砚，在汉代以前叫"研"，从字面意思来看，是研墨的工具。砚出现得非常早，从考古资料来看，最迟在新石器时代仰韶文化时期（距今7000—5000年）就已经出现人造砚。1980年，在陕西省临潼县一座仰韶文化初期墓葬中就出土了一套研墨工具。

汉代以前的砚，都配有一支研石棒，是用来研墨的。那时的墨是墨丸，不能单独用手握住，需要用研棒压住才能进行研磨。1975年，

> History of Inkstone

Inkstones have a long history. In the beginning, they were used together with a grounding stick. Inkstones are in many varieties and different materials, yet apart from stone, porcelain and jade, nowadays we can scarcely see inkstones made of other materials preserved in their pristine conditions.

The beginning

As suggested by its name in Chinese, inkstones are tools to make ink. Their appearance came fairly early, in the Yangshao Cultural Period of the Neolithic Age (7000-5000 years ago) at the latest. In 1980, a set of tools for ink making was discovered in a tomb in Lintong of Shaanxi Province from the early Yangshao Culture.

Before the Han Dynasty inkstones

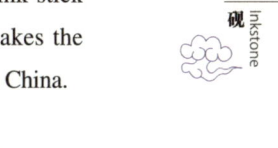

湖北云梦睡虎地秦墓出土了一方用鹅卵石加工制成的砚，砚形为圆饼形，其上无纹饰，配有研棒一支。同时出土的还有墨和笔，这是中国迄今发现的最早的书写砚。

- 颜料研磨器（仰韶文化）

这件研磨器带有盖，配有一支石质研磨棒，旁边有黑色的颜料。

Pigment grinder (Yangshao Culture, 7000-5000 years ago)

This grinder has a lid and a stick with black pigments nearby.

汉代时，砚的材质以石、陶为主，砚的使用已十分普遍，但大部分都配有研棒。直到东汉末年，墨的形制从墨丸改为可以手执的块墨，研棒才逐渐消失。这一时期，砚的形制也富于变化，常见的有圆形的石砚、龟形的陶砚等。

had a stick to go with for grinding ink balls, not sticks. The ball easily slipped away on the stone so keeping it in place by a stick was necessary. In 1975, an inkstone made from a pebble was unearthed from a Qin-dynasty tomb in Yunmeng of Hubei Province. It was round in shape, unornamented but had a grinding stick. Together with it were an ink stick and a writing brush. This set makes the oldest inkstone ever discovered in China.

- 石砚（秦）

Inkstone (Qin Dynasty, 221 B.C.-206 B.C.)

Inkstones of stone and pottery were popular during the Han Dynasty and they still went with a grinding stick. Grinding sticks existed until the late Eastern Han Dynasty when ink changed from balls to sticks that hands could hold easily. The shape of inkstone became diversified, the most common being round shape like a stone or pottery turtle.

• 石砚（汉）
Inkstone (Han Dynasty, 206 B.C.-220 A.D.)

• 盘龙石砚（汉）
Inkstone, Ornamented with Loong (Han Dynasty, 206 B.C.-220 A.D.)

魏晋南北朝时期的砚

魏晋南北朝时期，墨的形制不断改进，研磨棒因此彻底消失。砚的材质仍以陶、石为主。陶砚在南方盛行，多为圆形、箕形、长方形，并且都有蹄形砚足，使砚的高

Inkstones Made During the Wei, Jin, Southern and Northern Dynasties

Due to incessant improvements made during the Wei, Jin, Southern and Northern dynasties inkstones no longer needed grinding sticks, though their materials were still stone or pottery.

• 《北齐校书图》【局部】杨子华（北齐）
魏晋南北朝及隋唐时期的砚台有不少是仿辟雍（西周天子所设大学，其园如璧，四面环水）之形设计。砚台四周留有深槽储水，中心隆起，以众多的柱足承托砚身。

Proofreading (Partial) by Yang Zihua (Northern Qi Dynasty, 550-577)
Many inkstones were fashioned as minature replicas of the royal academy of the Western Zhou Dynasty, which was enclosed by a circular wall and had water around. Inkstones, had ditches to keep water along the four sides, central part higher and feet at the bottom to support the stone.

度增加。砚足的出现是为了适应当时席地坐和用矮几书写的要求。砚足还有三足、四足、五足、六足、八足之分。在中国北方地区则流行石砚，多为长方形和四方形，常在上面雕刻人物、花鸟等精美图案。

另外，魏晋南北朝时期的制砚工艺精进，金属砚、瓷砚、金砚、银砚等相继出现，这些材质名贵的砚大都做工十分精美。1957年，安徽省肥东县草庙乡大孤堆出土了一件南朝铜鎏金蟾蜍砚，砚上镶嵌着红、黄、蓝等各色宝石，此砚反映了魏晋南北朝时期制砚工艺的高超。

隋唐时期的砚

隋唐时期，由于书画纸的出现、毛笔与墨的精进，书画艺术取得卓越成就，砚的使用也更加广泛。

这一时期，一种陶制的"澄泥砚"大受欢迎，因其具有"含津益墨"的性能而著名。同时人们发现天然砚石的品质要好于人造的材质，在广东、安徽、甘肃、山东等地，都发现了大量制砚的名贵石料，产生了端砚、歙砚等名砚。除

Pottery ones were more common in China's south, mostly in round, rectangular or dustpan shape having feet to increase height. The feet were needed when writing while sitting on the floor or on a very low stool. The number of feet varied, from three to four, five, six and even eight. In China's north inkstones were popular, most being rectangular or square ornamented with carved human figures, birds or flowers.

By then, the workmanship has much improved, with new varieties available like metal, porcelain, gold or silver. Most of the inkstones were elaborately made. In 1957, in Feidong of Anhui Province, a bronze gilt inkstone from the Southern dynasties was brought to light, on which were inlaid precious stones in different colors. This inkstone showed the superb craftsmanship of the time.

Inkstones Made During the Sui and Tang Dynasties

Due to the invention of writing and painting paper, progress made in writing brushes and ink sticks and also because of a higher level of painting and calligraphy art reached, inkstones during the Sui and

了石材之外，还有其他特色材质的砚，如瓦当砚，其选材于秦汉魏晋时期废毁的宫殿残砖、剩瓦。晚唐五代时期，在北方还流行一种铁砚，砚身有柄，可执可握，发墨性能佳。

- 白釉辟雍砚（隋）
White Glazed Inkstone (Sui Dynasty, 581-618)

- 鸟纽辟雍盖砚（唐）
Inkstone with Feet and a Bird-knob Lid (Tang Dynasty, 618-907)

Tang dynasties gained a popularity it had never had before.

Pottery inkstones made from *Chengni* clay became popular because of their unusual ink-friendly property. People realized natural materials were better than man-made materials. In Guangdong, Anhui, Gansu and Shandong, nice materials for inkstones were found. Famous varieties like those made in Duanzhou and Shexian became known. Apart from stone, tile ends from ruined palaces of the Qin, Han, Wei and Jin dynasties became a much favored material. In the late Tang Dynasty or the Five dynasties that followed, in China's north, iron inkstones with a handle, convenient for holding and very ink-friendly, became a fashion.

Most of the inkstones during the Sui and Tang dynasties were either round or in the shape of dustpan. Most of them had no obvious concave to keep ink, simply having a side higher than the other for tidying brush tips. In Chinese, the character "dustpan" was quite like the character "phoenix". So inkstones in the shape of a dustpan were also called "phoenix inkstones". After the Tang Dynasty and the Five dynasties, taller furniture appeared.

隋唐时期，砚的造型以圆形和箕形为主，砚上没有砚堂和砚池，一侧砚足略高，使砚面略有斜倾，方便捺笔。箕形因与"凤"和"风"字形状相似，又称"凤（风）字砚"或"凤凰池"。唐末五代后，高型家具渐渐兴起，于是无足平台式的砚台开始流行，砚的形制也逐渐丰富起来。

So flat ink stones without feet became popular. Their shapes became more diversified.

砚池：又名"砚海"，指砚的低洼处，用来存积清水或墨汁。
Yanchi: it is the lower spot to keep water or ink.

砚岗：砚堂中间稍高的部分，四周成斜坡，使墨汁可以流向砚池。
Yangang: it is the ridge with a slope on all sides to make ink flow easily to Yanchi.

砚侧：砚的侧面，也可用作镌刻铭记之位。
Yance: it is the side of the inkstone, a possible place to receive inscriptions.

砚边：砚堂周围略高的边缘带。
Yanbian: it is the edge of Yantang, usually higher.

砚额：又名"砚头"，指砚的上部较其他三边更宽的部位，一般主要纹饰都安排在砚额。
Yan'e: it is also called the head, referring to the thicker side of the inkstone, often being the place to receive ornamentation.

砚背：砚的背面，又叫"砚底"，可用来镌刻铭记诗词。
Yanbei: it is the back or the bottom of the inkstone, likely to be inscribed with a poem.

砚堂：又名"墨堂"，为研墨之处。
Yantang: it is the spot to grind ink.

- 石砚（唐）
  Inkstone (Tang Dynasty, 618-907)

石砚的制作
The Making of a Inkstone

一方砚从砚石开采出来到制成成品，要经过选料、打磨、雕刻、配盒四个步骤。

From raw material to a completed inkstone there were many steps: material selection, carving, polishing and casing.

- 切割好的石坯
  The Cut Stone

- 四边整平的石坯
  The Stone that Has Been Polished on Sides

- 人工铲平的石坯（砚璞）
  The Stone that Has Been Polished Flat and Smooth, Now Called *Yanpu*.

选料：采出的砚石需要经过筛选，将瑕疵、裂痕、白皮、底板、顶板等部分剔除，保留"石肉"，然后对石料分等列级。根据石料的花纹进行巧妙的设计，做到"因石构图"，突出砚石的特色亮点，经过这一步加工的石坯称为"砚璞"。

Material selection: the stone material selected had to be scrutinized carefully to get rid of even the tiniest flaw. Only the best part in the middle was kept. Then, it was rated into different classes before a decorative pattern was designed to match the material's texture. Every stone was different and each had something unusual to be highlighted. By now, the stone was called Yan Pu, meaning "a selected stone to be worked on".

- 打磨
  Polishing

- 雕刻
  Carving

打磨：以油石和河沙磨砚璞，以去其凿口和刀路，然后用滑石打磨的工序。通过这一步可使砚石变得细腻、光滑。在经过浸墨润石、褪墨等工序处理后便能制成精良的砚石。

Polishing: this refers to the process of using very smooth stone and sand to polish, to get rid of any mark left from chiseling or cutting. Talc was used for polishp. After this the stone was to receive the last two steps: applying and removing ink for the first time.

雕刻：是对砚璞进行艺术处理与加工的工序。先要对砚石进行设计、创作，再运用深刀（高浮雕）、浅刀（低浮雕）、细刻、线刻等方法进行雕刻。

Carving: carving was to decorate the inkstone. The design made was transferred onto the stone by cutting knives in high or low relief. Line carving or detail carving was common.

配盒：精美的砚都要配上匣盒，以起到防尘和保护砚石的作用。砚盒一般都是木制的，而且多选用名贵木材。砚盒的造型依照砚石的形状而定。

Casing: a fine inkstone must be cased to keep it from dust. Usually a case was made of wood of an expensive kind in the shape that matched the inkstone.

- 雕刻好的砚台
  The Carved Inkstone

宋元时期的砚

自宋代开始，砚就以石砚为主导，开发出了更多可用于制砚的新石料，如淄州金雀石、高唐州紫石、宿州乐石、登州石、戎州石、泸州石、蔡州白石等。石砚受到重视，一方面是因为它的发墨效果好，符合书画艺术家对研墨的高要求，另一方面是文人对砚石本身的色彩、纹理也产生了浓厚的兴趣。韩琦、蔡襄、王安石、苏轼、苏

Inkstones Made During the Song and Yuan Dynasties

From the Song Dynasty, apart from old types of stone for making inkstones, new ones like *Jinque* from Zizhou, *Zishi* from Gaotang, *Leshi* from Suzhou and the stones from Dengzhou, Rongzhou, Luzhou and Caizhou were valued. One reason for their popularity was their ink-friendliness which met artists' need for ink grinding; another reason was the favorable remarks from literary giants

辙、黄庭坚等宋代文豪都写过不少赞美石砚色彩、花纹的诗篇。

• 抄手石砚（宋）
Inkstone (Song Dynasty, 960-1279)

宋代时，石砚的造型也更加多样化。如歙砚就有月、圭、莲叶、古钱、蟾蜍、琴、辟雍、凤字等四十余种造型。当时文人还热衷于为石砚制作铭文，镌刻在砚的侧面或砚底、砚盖、砚屏上，由此开了后世

• 蝉形歙砚（宋）
Cicada-shaped Inkstone, Shexian Style (Song Dynasty, 960-1279)

like Han Qi, Cai Xiang, Wang Anshi, Su Shi … on these stones' unique color and texture. The poems they wrote excited the public.

• 玉带砚（宋）
Jade Ribbon Inkstone (Song Dynasty, 960-1279)

More shapes appeared during the Song Dynasty, and in the *She* school some inkstones were fashioned after plants, animals, musical instruments, royal academy of the Western Zhou Dynasty, written characters … Scholars had a strong interest in inscribing the stone. Carvings might appear on the sides, bottom, lid and body of a inkstone. Later generations followed, as was seen during the Yuan Dynasty, a very bold but simple was seen in many designs. It was during this time that a unique kind called *Nuanyan*, or "heatable inkstone" appeared. This type had a place reserved on its lower part to be heated from fire, to keep

书写砚铭的先河。元代则将粗犷的民族特色注入砚的造型中，体现出朴拙的时代风格。此时还出现了暖砚，制砚时工匠在砚台下部留出空间，可置火加热，防止墨液冻结。

宋代还出现了有关砚的专著，如苏易简的《文房四谱》中的《砚谱》、米芾的《砚史》、唐积的《歙州砚谱》等。

ink from freezing.

Writings about inkstones appeared during the Song Dynasty like the "Inkstone Chapter" in *Wenfang Sipu*, or *The Four Treasures of the Study* by Su Yijian, *History of Inkstones* by Mi Fu and *Varieties of Inkstones from Shezhou* by Tang Ji.

• 陶箕形砚（元）
Pottery Dustpan-shape Inkstone (Yuan Dynasty, 1206-1368)

欧阳修与歙、端二砚

欧阳修（1007—1072），庐陵（今江西省吉安）人，宋代著名文学家、史学家，他是爱砚之人。

欧阳修平时用的砚台是端砚，自从结识欧阳徽后，改用歙砚。欧阳徽送给欧阳修一方双龙戏珠金星砚。此砚星光闪闪，手感柔嫩润滑，欧阳修爱不释手，赞其为"宝砚"。

Ouyang Xiu with *She* and *Duan* Style Inkstones

Ouyang Xiu (1007-1072), a native from Luling (present-day Ji'an of Jiangxi Province), a famous Song writer and historian, also a famed inkstone lover.

After he came to know Ouyang Hui, Ouyang Xiu switched from *Duan* style inkstone to a *She* style one. The teahouse owner gave him an inkstone with shining stars on surface and ornamentation of two loongs playing with a pearl. The inkstone felt very soft, tender and smooth. Ouyang Xiu took it as a treasure.

米芾索砚

米芾（1051—1107），宋代著名的书画家、鉴赏家、收藏家，性格狂放。他能诗文、擅书画，精于鉴赏，爱好收藏。

米芾爱砚至深。一次宋徽宗让米芾到宫中写字，并让他使用御桌上的方砚。米芾写完后，手捧御砚，对皇帝说："此砚我已用过，皇上不能再用，就将砚给我吧。"宋徽宗就将砚赐给了他。米芾随即将砚台装入怀中，跑回家去。

米芾不仅爱砚、藏砚，还不断地加以研究，著有《砚史》一书，书中对各种砚台的产地、色泽、细润、工艺都做了论述。

Mi Fu Asked for an Inkstone

Mi Fu, (1051-1107), was a Song-dynasty painter, calligrapher, art connoisseur and collector, a man who refused to be bound by conventional ideas. Yet his attainments in literary writing, painting, calligraphy, artistic criticism and art collection were amazing.

His love for inkstones was legendary. Once, he was sent by Emperor Huizong to do calligraphy in the palace. He was allowed to use the emperor's square inkstone on the desk. After he finished writing he held the inkstone in hand. "I have used this one," said him, "so it is improper for your majesty to use it again. Why not give it to me?" At this, the emperor granted his request. Mi Fu instantly pocketed the inkstone and ran back home as fast as his legs could take him.

Not only a lover and a collector, Mi Fu was also a researcher who wrote *The History of Inkstones*, in which he detailed different varieties, their places of production, unique characteristics and different making technologies.

• 米芾像
Mi Fu

明清时期的砚

明清时期，砚的发展达到顶峰，出现了很多精雕细琢的精品砚。明代时，对砚石的质地要求更高。为了得到上乘的砚石，人们重新发掘被水淹没多年的端石老坑，发现了比前代更为优质且细润美丽的石头。文人们赋予这些砚石以美名，如青花、蕉叶白、冰纹、鱼脑冻等。

在这一时期，砚雕艺术人才辈出，雕刻技术和制作工艺都达到历史最高水平，出现众多的砚雕流派。江南的砚雕图纹清秀隽永，做工高雅脱俗，人称"浙派"；广

Inkstones Made During the Ming and Qing Dynasties

Inkstones making technology peaked during the Ming and Qing dynasties with many master works appearing. People of the Ming Dynasty put a higher demand on stone quality. In order to get a quality inkstone people dug into old mining pits flooded by water for years, where they found stones of even better quality. Scholars named these stones after the textures they had.

This period of history saw master makers with legendary skills. Also, different schools appeared: those made in south of the Yangtze River, described as "Zhejiang school", featured nice

- 雕人物端砚（清）
  Duan Inkstone Carved with Human Figure (Qing Dynasty, 1616-1911)

东、福建的砚雕纹饰丰满，图案繁复，人称"广作"；宫廷用砚材料考究，做工规整，带有一股富贵气，被称为"官作"。另外，文人用砚以风雅见长，往往透出一种书卷气；民间用砚因注重实用，不太讲究材质与做工，风格质朴。这些不同地区、不同风格的砚雕最终汇成了砚雕艺术的三大流派——粤派、徽派和苏派。晚清民国时期又出现了海派，使得砚雕工艺更加灿烂。

workmanship and patterns of elegant simplicity; those made in Guangdong and Fujian, described as "Guangdong style", showed impressive decoration in the noble and luxurious motif; inkstones made for royal use were called "palatial style"; inkstones for scholars showed a graceful academic pursuit, while the inkstones for common people were simple and practical in use, usually made of ordinary material and in plain style. Together, they made three schools of the time: the Guangdong, Jiangsu and Anhui schools. In the late Qing Dynasty or during the early years of the Minguo Period, a new school appeared in Shanghai to make it four.

- 宜兴雕龙砚（清）
Inkstone with Loong, Made in Yixing (Qing Dynasty, 1616-1911)

明清时期的砚雕流派
Popular Carving Styles During the Ming and Qing Dynasties

粤派砚雕艺术

粤派以端砚雕为代表,其风格形成于明代,俗称"广作"。雕刻手法以细刻、线刻和浅浮雕为主,适当穿插深刀雕刻,以花鸟、鱼虫、走兽、山水、人物、仿古器皿、龙凤瑞兽、秋叶、棉豆、玉兰等喜庆吉祥题材为主,形象生动,富有变化。

The Guangdong Style

Represented by *Duan* inkstones, the Guangdong style appearing in the Ming Dynasty(1368-1644) featured highly exquisite line or low relief carvings. This style also had some, though not many, high reliefs of life-like human figures, owers, birds, animals, antiques, crops and plants, all being auspicious symbols.

- 龙凤砚(清)
Loong and Phoenix Inkstone (Qing Dynasty, 1616-1911)

徽派砚雕艺术

徽派以歙砚雕为代表,雕刻以浮雕浅刻为主,间或出现深刀雕刻,不做立体的镂空雕,手法细腻,层次分明。徽派砚雕构图多方圆规整,砚边多宽厚,常饰以传统纹样和各种变异纹饰,使得整个砚的造型雍容大方,格调简明。

The Anhui Style

Represented by *She* inkstones, this style featured low relief carving or occasional high relief works, but had never three-dimensional hollow-outs, all conducted exquisitely to show images arranged on different layers. Most of the *She* inkstones are of neat square or round shapes. Their thick sides often had traditional lines as decoration, having a simple yet graceful beauty.

- 歙石长方形砚(明)
Rectangular *She* Inkstone (Ming Dynasty, 1368-1644)

苏派砚雕艺术

苏派砚雕追求平淡、雅逸的风格，表现高雅古典之气，讲求刀法的精致，其构图疏朗，意境高远。苏派砚以随形砚为主，追求简朴古雅、自然华美的艺术境界。

The Jiangsu-style Carving

This style featured simple elegance and profound message, exquisite carving technique to convey a noble aspiration. Patterns carved often followed the shape of the inkstone. Elegant simplicity and a refined taste made the key words of this style.

- 碧玉"莲叶"随形砚（清）
Green Jade Inkstone of Lotus Leaves (Qing Dynasty, 1616-1911)

海派砚雕

晚清民国时期，上海地区出现了以写实为主要风格的砚雕流派，史称"海派砚雕"。制砚以仿自然物体为主，如鸟兽、草虫、花果及古钟、蘑菇等，精工巧妙，写实性极强。

The Shanghai Style

Shanghai style appearing during the late Qing Dynasty and the Minguo Period showed a realism pursuit. Most of its subjects were natural things in life like birds, animals, grass and insects, flowers and fruits, ancient bells and mushroom, all rendered highly realistic in great detail.

- 端石瓜瓞砚（清）
Duan Inkstone (Qing Dynasty, 1616-1911)

> 古砚的种类

　　按照材质的不同，古砚可以分为石砚、泥陶砚、瓷砚、漆木砚、玉砚、金属砚等，其中以石砚为主流。

　　石砚取材于天然石料，多是江河中常年被雨水冲刷的石头。石砚自汉代起才开始应用，唐代时盛行并广泛运用起来，明清时期达到顶峰。尽管石砚出现的时间与泥陶砚、瓷砚等相比较晚，但石砚的品

> Varieties of Antique Inkstone

In terms of materials, ancient inkstones were made of stone, pottery, clay, porcelain, lacquered wood, jade and metal, but the majority were stone.

Inkstones came from the stones after being washed by rainwater for years. Earliest inkstones appeared during the Han Dynasty, were popular during the Tang Dynasty and reached pinnacle during the Ming and Qing dynasties.

- 石砚（唐）
Inkstone (Tang Dynasty, 618-907)

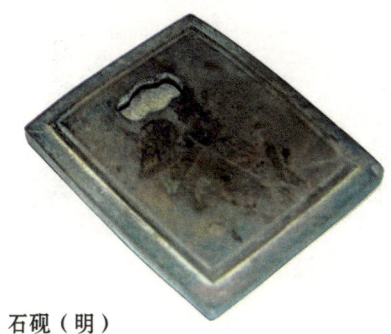

- 石砚（明）
Inkstone (Ming Dynasty, 1368-1644)

质居于众砚之首，是最受欢迎，也是收藏最热的砚台品种。

泥陶砚是唐代以前使用最多的砚，由于泥陶砚较易破碎，所以存世者极少，比较著名的有汉代"十二峰陶砚"、唐代的"二十二柱足圆陶砚"，均收藏于故宫博物院。泥陶砚包括陶砚、澄泥砚、瓦砚、砖砚、缸砚、紫砂砚等类型。

• 瓦当砚（汉）
Tile-end Inkstone (Han Dynasty, 206 B.C.-220 A.D.)

• 福禄寿澄泥砚（现代）
Cheng-clay Inkstone of Happiness, Officialdom and Longevity (Modern Times)

Though younger than pottery, clay and porcelain ones, stone had every reason to top others as the most popular, most collectable and most sought-after one.

The clay-pottery inkstones were popular before the Tang Dynasty but because of their fragility very few have come down in history. Among the existant ones were "12-peak inkstone" from the Han Dynasty and "22-feet round inkstone" from the Tang Dynasty, both now in the collection of the Palace Museum. Other kinds of this variety were pottery, clay, tile, brick, vat or *Zisha* (boccaro, or simply purple clay).

Porcelain inkstones first appeared during the Wei and Jin dynasties and were seen in all later dynasties. Apart from the spot for grinding ink, it was glazed by fire. During the Ming and Qing dynasties, due to fully-fledged firing technology some famous porcelain inkstones were made, many bearing the year of making and the names of the workshop and the maker, thus of high artistic value. Because of their hardness and less ink-friendliness, they were more often for display than for practical use.

Lacquered wood inkstones were in a color bearing closeness to the *Chengni*, almost as nice as stone ones. This kind

瓷砚最早出现于魏晋时期，此后历代皆有制作。瓷砚除砚堂中间的研墨处外全身上釉，然后以高温烧结而成。明清时期，陶瓷烧制技术的发展使得精品瓷砚大量生产，砚上多留有制作时间、作坊名称及工匠姓名等，极具艺术性。瓷砚因其瓷胎过硬，磨墨时不易下墨，实用性较差，故多作观赏陈设之用。

漆木砚是用木材为胎，再以生漆髹成砚堂而制成的砚。其色似澄泥，可与石砚媲美。漆木砚在清代曾风靡一时。

玉砚是以玉制作的砚。由于玉的硬度高，雕琢比石砚、陶砚困难，所以玉砚大多形制简单。玉砚质地细腻、坚实，但因其不发墨、不吸水，实用性不强，故只作抿笔和收藏之用。

金属砚以金、银、铜、铁、锡等金属制成，以铜砚较为常见。金属砚不常用于书写。

- 褐釉兽座箕形瓷砚（唐）
Glazed Brown Animal Inkstone, Porcelain (Tang Dynasty, 618-907)

of inkstones was popular during the Qing Dynasty.

Jade inkstones took jade as the material. But because of the toughness of jade, which was more difficult to craft than other kinds, most jade inkstones were in a simple shape. They were hard, fine in texture, and absorbed less ink or water, so less practical in use. They were only for collection or tidying brush tips.

Metal inkstones took gold, silver, bronze, iron or tin as materials, mainly in bronze. Seldom was a metal inkstone in use.

- 青玉鹅式砚（清）
Goose Inkstone, Gray Jade (Qing Dynasty, 1616-1911)

砚的基本形制
Basic Forms

砚的形制多种多样，为文房增添了不少情趣。主要形制有几何形砚、动物形砚、植物形砚、箕形砚、抄手砚、圈足砚、随形砚、暖砚等。

Inkstones in different shapes made a study room tasteful. Common ones were of geometric, animal or plant shapes, dustpan shape, handled or feeted, some following the shape of the material, and some could be heated.

几何形砚是指形状为圆形、椭圆形、长方形、方形、八角形等规则形状的砚台，其中方形砚和长方形砚最为常见。

The geometrical shape included round, oval, rectangular, square or octagonal shapes. Of them all, the square and rectangular were the most common ones.

- 端石灵芝长方砚（清）

Rectangular *Duan* Inkstone with Polyporus Lucidus
(Qing Dynasty, 1616-1911)

动物形砚是以动物为形制的砚，题材以神兽形象的动物为多，寓意吉祥，也有一些以现实中的动物为题材的，如牛形砚、鹅式砚、鱼形砚等。

Legendary animals were favored images for inkstone making because of the auspicious message they carried. Some resembled animals in real life, like ox, goose or fish.

- 澄泥卧牛形砚（明）

Ox Inkstone, *Chengni* (Ming Dynasty, 1368-1644)

植物形砚是模仿某些植物形状的砚，常见的有竹节砚、蕉叶砚、荷叶砚、荔枝砚、蘑菇砚等。

Plant shape inkstones took the shapes of bamboo joints, banana or lotus leaves, litchi or mushrooms.

- 白玉荷叶式砚（清）
  Lotus-leaf Inkstone, White Jade (Qing Dynasty, 1616-1911)

箕形砚形同簸箕，砚底一端落地，一端以足支撑，砚面倾斜，便于聚墨。箕形砚流行于唐代。

Dustpan inkstones had one side resting on desk and a leg on the other side for support, thus making a slope for ink to flow and gather. This shape was popular during the Tang Dynasty.

- 箕形砚（唐）
  Dustpan Inkstone (Tang Dynasty, 618-907)

抄手砚由箕形砚演变而来，砚面一端低，一端高，底挖空，因可用手抄砚底而得名。抄手砚较轻便，始于五代时期，盛行于宋代。

Chaoshou inkstone got its name from its unique shape: one side high, the other side low and its bottom hollowed; easy to handle by grasping its bottom. Light in weight, this kind first appeared during the Five dynasties and gained popularity during the Song Dynasty.

- 抄手砚（宋）
  Chaoshou Inkstone (Song Dynasty, 960-1279)

圈足砚指砚面呈圆形，以多脚围绕作砚足支撑砚面的砚。砚足的形状有兽蹄、兽首等形状。圈足砚流行于唐代以前，是为了适应当时在矮桌上书写而制作的。

Multiple-feet inkstones had round and multiple feet at the bottom shaped like animal claws or heads. This variety, popular before Tang, was designed for writing on a very low table.

• 圈足砚（唐）
Multiple-feet Inkstone (Tang Dynasty, 618-907)

随形砚指因材而制，不在乎砚的轮廓外形，只借助砚材的纹理而创作、雕琢的砚。随形砚奇巧而有灵气，流行甚广，尤以随形扁砚最多，造型千姿百态。

Suixing inkstones: *Suixing* meant the inkstones were made following the shape and textures of the material. This kind was tremendously popular for its unique charm. The flat ones were the predominate style.

• 歙石金星随形砚（清）
Suixing Inkstone with Golden Stars from Shezhou (Qing Dynasty, 1616-1911)

暖砚有两种形式：一种是在墨堂下凿出空腔，灌注热水于内，以保持砚面的温度；另一种是在砚面之下设置底座，底座多为金属制成砚匣，可置炭火以保持温度。金属匣一般都精雕巧作，别具一格。暖砚盛行于明清时期，暖砚砚面多为歙石、端石和松花江石。

Heated inkstones had two kinds: one had warm water in the hollow under its ink pool to keep ink warm; the other had an elaborately wrought metal stand at the bottom to hold charcoal. Heated inkstones, popular during the Qing Dynasty, often used the stones from Shezhou, Duanzhou and the Songhua River.

> 四大名砚

　　四大名砚之说，最早见于宋人苏易简所著《文房四谱·砚谱》："砚有四十余品，以青州红丝石为第一，端州斧柯山石为第二，歙州龙尾石为第三，甘肃洮河石为第四。"后来，红丝石因开采枯竭而被澄泥砚所取代。

> The Most Famous Four Varieties

The saying of the most famous four was first seen in Su Yijian's book, in its chapter about inkstones, "Inkstones are in over forty varieties, but the stone with red threads on it from Qingzhou being the best, the stone from Fuke Mount of Duanzhou the second, the stone from Longwei of Shezhou the third and the stone from the Taohe River of Gansu, the fourth." Later, after the red-thread stone resource was exhausted, the *Chengni* inkstone took its place.

红丝砚

红丝砚在宋代居四大名砚之首,产于青州(今山东潍坊、益都、淄博一带),其特点是色泽明艳雅丽,红黄相间,石纹旋曲如波云,石质细润易发墨。红丝石在唐代享有盛名,但到宋代便已采尽,故传世实物极少。宋代苏易简在《文房四谱》中将红丝砚列为第一,是当时最佳的砚品。

The Red-thread Inkstone

Topping the famous four, this red-thread inkstone came from Qingzhou (present-day Weifang, Yidu and Zibo), featuring bright colors of red and yellow, with twirling and tumbling textures like clouds, very fine, smooth and ink-friendly. It was taken as a treasure during the Tang Dynasty. However, by the Song Dynasty no more resource was left. Very few exist today. In his book, Su Yijian listed it as the best of all under the heaven.

- 红丝石
  The Red-thread Stone

- 红丝石砚(清)
  Red-thread Inkstone (Qing Dynasty, 1616-1911)

端砚

端砚因产于端州（今广东肇庆）而得名，最早出现于隋末唐初。端砚石质温润，纹理缜密，贮水不涸，磨之无声，溜不损毫。端砚利于发墨，石品（天然花纹）上佳，经过精雕细琢之后具有极高的艺术价值。

Duan Inkstones

This variety got its name from Duanzhou where its material came from (today's Zhaoqing). It was first known during the late Sui or the early Tang dynasties. *Duan* stones featured fine texture and closely knitted veins, very ink-friendly and fit for keeping water. It gave no sound when the ink stick was ground on it. The best made ones boasted high artistic value.

- 端石云蝠砚（清）
  Duan Inkstone with Cloud Veins (Qing Dynasty, 1616-1911)

- 端石九眼方砚（清）
  Duan Inkstone with Nine Holes (Qing Dynasty, 1616-1911)

端砚的著名石品

石品是划分砚石不同品种的依据之一，端砚的石品通过花纹来鉴别，有以下几种著名石品。

青花 紫色石砚中的最佳品类，其上散布有细小的蓝色花纹或斑点。这些花纹或斑点隐在紫石之中，浸入水中才能看到。

鱼脑冻 砚石中的图案像受冻的鱼脑，有聚有散，洁白如晴天的白云，好像风一吹就要散开，松散如一团柳絮，仿佛一触就要动起来。鱼脑冻是端石精品中最名贵的石品。

蕉叶白 又称"蕉白"，形如蕉叶初展，似含露欲滴，洁白细嫩。蕉叶白四周定有火捺纹（像用火烙过的痕迹），两者相伴而生。蕉叶白石质嫩软细腻，滑如肌肤，利于发墨，是端砚中的上品。

火捺　又称"火烙",颜色如火烙一般,紫红中带微黑。火捺中最名贵的是金钱火捺,形状为圆形或椭圆形。

天青　指纯洁无杂色、无瑕疵的端石,较为难得。

冰纹　也叫"冰纹冻",端石的花纹形状像冰冻裂,属于一般品种。

翡翠　也叫青脉,砚石表面有绿色圆点或短纹。

绿端　砚石青绿微黄,是端石中非常少见的珍品,易发墨。

荡　指多种品类集于一体的端石。"荡"就是"湖",湖中多种动植物并生,因此得名。上等荡石里层是鱼脑冻,冻内为青花,冻外是蕉叶白,蕉叶白外是火捺纹围绕。荡石难得一见,是端石中的名贵品种。

Famous Varieties of *Duan* Inkstones

Stone quality determined the class of the inkstone. *Duan* stones had the following varieties:

Qinghua, or pale green flower, the best of *Duan* stones. In purple color, it got its name from very fine blue veins or dots only visible in water.

Yunaodong or frozen fish brain, having continuous or disparate veins, like clouds in the sky drifting with wind. This variety was the rarest in *Duan* stones.

Jiaoyebai or fresh banana leaf: this variety got its name from its veins like fresh and tender banana leaves; around the veins were marks like left by fire. This variety gave a very tender and fine look, like woman's beautiful skin. Also ink-friendly, this variety was a very expensive kind in the *Duan* stone family.

Huona or marks left by fire: dark purple, almost black. The rarest stone in this variety was called *Jinqian Huona* in round or oval shape.

Tianqing or heavenly blue: the stones without any flaw in it, very rare to get.

Bingwen or ice vein: having veins like tiny cracks found in ice, a common variety.

Feicui or emerald: also called the blue vein, having green dots or short veins on surface.

Lvduan or green ends: pale green, a bit yellowish, very rare in the *Duan* family, also ink-friendly.

Dang: referring to a stone having all kinds of veins mentioned above on surface, one next to another like a lake overgrown with varieties of plants. This variety was very rare.

• 鱼脑冻砚(清)

鱼脑冻因砚石中的图案像受冻的鱼脑而得名,是端石精品中的精品。

Yunaodong Inkstone (Qing Dynasty, 1616-1911)

It got the name because the pattern is like some frozen fish brain. This piece is the best of the best of the *Duan* style inkstones.

歙砚

歙砚也称"龙尾砚",唐代始有,因砚石产于歙州而得名。歙砚石的特点是石色青莹,纹理细密,发墨既快速又细润。歙砚因其石组织结构聚结紧密,自然孔隙小,故具有发墨益毫、滑不拒墨、涩不滞笔、贮墨久而不涸的特点。

She Inkstones

She Inkstones were also called *Longwei* or the tail of loong inkstones, first seen during the Tang Dynasty. They got their name from the stones quarried in Shezhou. The stones from there were in a very pleasant color, very solid and very fine in texture, smooth and ink friendly. Because of their solid nature and exceptionally tiny apertures, they are able to keep ink fresh and fluid for a long time.

- 歙砚(现代)
  The *She* Inkstone (Modern Times)

- 龙尾砚
  The Loong-tail Inkstone

洮河砚

洮河砚又叫"绿石砚",因产于洮州(今甘肃临潭)而得名。洮河石深埋于大河深水之底,因山陡水险,气候冷,不易开采;洮州又远居陇上,交通不便,所以洮河砚在明清时期已属珍品。洮河石属沉积岩,质细色美,发墨快,温润无比,可呵气成珠,以其制成的砚,余墨贮于其中经月不涸,亦不变质,前人有"端州歙州无此色"的说法。

Taohe Inkstones

The *Taohe* inkstones had another name, "green inkstones". They got the name from the place where the stone was quarried, Taozhou (present-day Lintan of Gansu), from the bottom of the deep Taohe River. Quarrying was very difficult because of the cold weather, torrential waves and difficult transportation. Even during the Qing Dynasty the inkstones made with this *Taohe* stone were rare. This stone, a sedimentary kind, had a very fine texture in a beautiful look, perfect for grinding. Also, it was said exhaled air tured into water drops the instant it touched the stone surface. Ink in it remained fresh and uid after months. No wonder people said, "This inkstone could not find its match from either Duanzhou or Shezhou ".

• 洮河石砚(清)
Taohe Inkstone (Qing Dynasty, 1616-1911)

• 洮河石长方砚(明)
Rectangular *Taohe* Inkstone (Ming Dynasty, 1368-1644)

澄泥砚

　　澄泥砚是陶砚中的精品，后取代红丝砚成中国四大名砚之一。澄泥砚始于晋、唐之间，早于端砚、歙砚。澄泥砚产于山西省绛县，具有细腻坚实、滋润胜水、历寒不冰、发墨不损毫的特点，能与石质佳砚相媲美。

　　澄泥砚是将细河泥经过仔细淘洗、过滤后逐渐沉淀于袋中，经年后取出风干，掺进黄丹团后用力揉搓，放入模具成型，然后用竹刀雕

Chengni Inkstones

A pottery variety, the *Chengni* inkstone replaced the famous red-thread to be one of the famous four. First seen during the Jin Dynasty or the Tang Dynasty, earlier than the *Duan* or *She* inkstones, the *Chengni* inkstones made in Jiangxian County, Shanxi, were solid in texture, pleasantly smooth and never froze even in the coldest weather. Though made in clay, they were as good as stone ones.

　　Fine river mud was washed, rinsed and sieved repeatedly before it

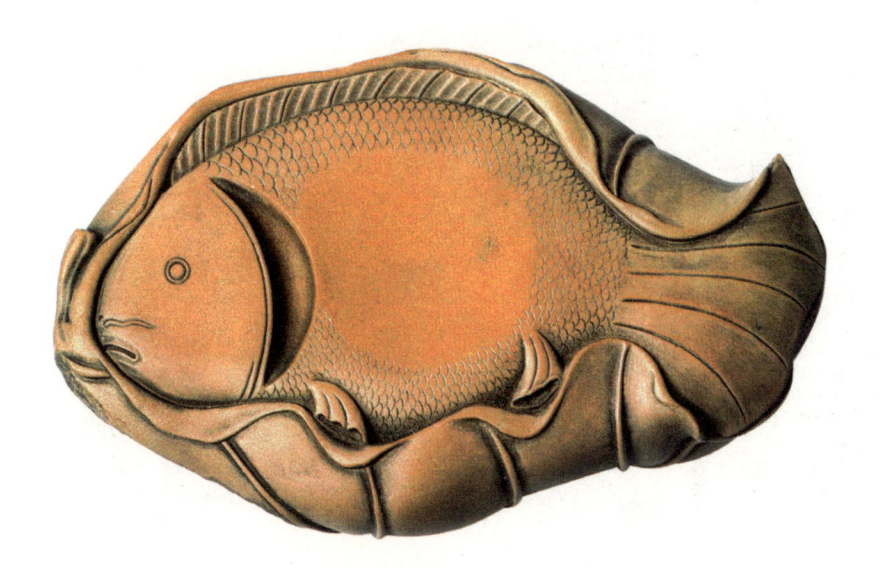

- 荷叶鲤鱼澄泥砚（现代）
Lotus and Carp *Chengni* Inkstone (Modern Times)

琢，干燥后放进窑内烧，最后裹上黑蜡烧制而成。

　　澄泥砚因原料来源、烧制时间的不同而具有鳝鱼黄、蟹壳青、绿豆砂、玫瑰紫、豆瓣砂、朱砂等不同颜色。澄泥砚一般注重图案，讲究造型，雕砚刀笔凝练，技艺精湛，状物摹态形象毕肖、灵通活脱。

accumulated in a cloth bag. Years later, after the mud was air-dried, yellow lead was added, and the mixture was kneaded until it was ready for molding. After receiving a decoration from a bamboo cutter, it was air-dried, coated with black wax and fired in a kiln.

　　Because of the different places the clay came from and the different time of kilning, the *Chengni* inkstones took different colors, yellow, pale green, purple or red, very impressive after carving. Every image carved was exquisite and life-like.

- 九龙澄泥砚（现代）
Nine-loong *Chengni* Inkstone (Modern Times)

古砚的保养

砚的历史悠久，古代中国人在使用过程中已形成了很好的收藏和保存砚的方法。

仔细洗砚：砚使用后，应随时洗涤，不能留墨，以免因墨干燥龟裂而损坏砚面。洗砚要用清水和皂角水，不可用碱水，因碱水有微腐蚀性，久用会使砚石变得平光而无法发墨。洗砚时将砚置于木盆内（不能用水泥盆、瓷盆洗涤，以免碰伤砚），用经水泡软后的丝瓜瓤慢慢洗涤，这样既能洗去墨垢，又不伤砚。

古人认为长期洗涤的砚，时间一久，还会出现轻微的光泽，流露出一种古雅之色，这就是行家们所珍视的"包浆"。

以水养砚：砚洗干净以后，还得用清水保养。将洗涤干净的砚取出风干，然后放于砚匣内。在砚池中注入清水，每日一换，以养砚之莹润。

以匣藏砚：藏砚最好用木制的砚匣。

注意避光：藏砚一定要注意避光，否则砚质易干燥，也易使砚匣干裂。

- 带盒长方形端砚（清）
Cased Rectangular *Duan* Inkstone (Qing Dynasty, 1616-1911)

The Keeping of Ancient Inkstones

Over the past thousands of years Chinese people have developed an effective way to keep inkstones out of harm's way.

Washed carefully after use: after being used, an inkstone should be washed clean immediately. No ink should be left after use, which might dry up and damage the inkstone. Washing should be done with clean water plus saponin, no water containing soda to be used because it was erosive and after a period of time the inkstone might become glossy and repellent against ink. Washing should be done inside a wood basin (no hard basin like porcelain or cement because damage may happen from knocks). Use a vegetable sponge and do washing gently. That soft stuff gets rid of ink effectively and leaves no stain.

After years of washing in the right way, ancient people believed, inkstones might take on a shimmering look, something only antiques had. Experts called this change *Baojiang*.

Use water to moisten inkstones: after being washed clean, fresh water is used for further care. Then, the inkstone is left to air-dry before put back to its case. A little fresh water should be left in its ink pool and changed every day.

Use a case to keep it: wood cases are the best.

Keep them out of the sun: this is important. Otherwise, inkstones may dry and the case crack.

• 三星五福石砚（清）

Inkstone with Three Stars upon Five Bats Pattern (An Auspicious Design Implied Wealth, Longevity, Luck and Happiness) (Qing Dynasty, 1616-1911)

附录：其他文房用具
Appendix: Other Tools in a Traditional Chinese Study

笔筒

用于盛放毛笔的筒状物，形状多样，以圆筒状最为常见，外壁常雕刻精美纹饰。笔筒的材质很多，有竹、木、象牙、玉石、瓷、雕漆、金属等。

Writing Brush Container

Containers for writing brushes were in different shapes but the most common one was cylindrical, often carved on their outside walls. They were made with materials like bamboo, wood, ivory, jade, marble, porcelain, lacquer or metal.

- 竹雕梅花笔筒（明）
  Bamboo Brush Container with Plum Blossoms (Ming Dynasty, 1368-1644)

- 紫檀云龙笔筒（清）
  Rosewood Brush Container with Cloud and Loong (Qing Dynasty, 1616-1911)

- 黄釉竹节雕春牛图笔筒（清）
Yellow Glazed Bamboo Joint Brush Container with Ox (Qing Dynasty, 1616-1911)

- 碧玉九老图笔筒（清）
Jade Brush Container with Sages (Qing Dynasty, 1616-1911)

- 象牙雕笔筒（清）
Carved Ivory Brush Container (Qing Dynasty, 1616-1911)

- 蓝上蓝墨彩花鸟纹海棠式笔筒（清）
Glazed Crabapple Blue Brush Container with Auspicious Images (Qing Dynasty, 1616-1911)

• 粉彩开光石纹笔筒（清）
Color Stone Brush Container (Qing Dynasty, 1616-1911)

• 牛骨雕笔筒（现代）
Carved Ox Bone Brush Container (Modern Times)

笔架

用于临时搁放毛笔的文房用具。使用毛笔时，因笔头蘸有墨，在放下时需保证笔头悬空，不会来回滚动，笔架因此而诞生。笔架没有固定的形状，一般多为三峰或多峰，有的钻有透孔。

Writing Brush Rack

For temporary rest of writing brushes. When a brush tip had ink on it, it must be placed without touching anything when temporarily out of use. The rack was also to prevent a brush from rolling on the desk. Brush racks had no fixed shape, but were often made for three or more brushes. Some had holes.

• 青花笔架（明）
Blue-and-white Brush Rack (Ming Dynasty, 1368-1644)

• 白玉笔架（清）
White Jade Brush Rack (Qing Dynasty, 1616-1911)

- 青玉凤凰松树笔架（清）
Gray Jade Brush Rack with Phoenix and Pine Tree (Qing Dynasty, 1616-1911)

- 青玉鹿纹笔架（清）
Gray Jade Deer Brush Rack (Qing Dynasty, 1616-1911)

- 五峰铜笔架（清）
Five-peak Copper Brush Rack (Qing Dynasty, 1616-1911)

- 青花五峰笔架（清）
Blue-and-white Five-peak Brush Rack (Qing Dynasty, 1616-1911)

- 黄杨木天然笔架（清）
Boxwood Brush Rack (Qing Dynasty, 1616-1911)

笔洗

洗毛笔的容器。古人用毛笔蘸墨写字，因墨中含有胶，墨干后会把毛笔的毛粘住，再用水泡开时，会损伤毛笔。所以一般不用毛笔时，都在笔洗中把毛笔洗净。绘画时因为使用墨、颜料的不同，也要用笔洗，所以笔洗是不可缺少的文具。

笔洗形制奇巧，样式繁多，多为大口或敞口的浅容器，常见的有荷叶式、贝叶式、葵瓣式、蕉叶式、瓜式、葫芦式、凤式等样式的笔洗。

Writing Brush Washer

It is a container for washing brushes. Because ink contained glue that held the brush hairs together, when the ink was dry, damage may happen to brush tips. Each time after use, the brush tip had to be washed clean—the same with tips dipped paints. Therefore, writing brush washers became indispensable.

These washers might have different forms but most of them had a big opening on top. They were shaped like lotus, pattra, sunflower, banana leaf, a melon or a gourd.

- 青玉福寿花形洗（明）

Gray Jade Flower Writing Brush Washer with Longevity and Happiness Symbols (Ming Dynasty, 1368-1644)

- 墨玉椭圆梅花洗（明）

Black Jade Oval Plum Writing Brush Washer (Ming Dynasty, 1368-1644)

- 青玉叶形洗（明）

Gray Jade Leaf Writing Brush Washer (Ming Dynasty, 1368-1644)

- 仿痕玉活环菊花洗（清）

Jade Chrysanthemum Writing Brush Washer (Qing Dynasty, 1616-1911)

• 白玉荷叶洗（清）
White Jade Lotus Leaf Writing Brush Washer (Qing Dynasty, 1616-1911)

• 白玉荷莲笔洗（清）
White Jade Lotus Leaf Writing Brush Washer (Qing Dynasty, 1616-1911)

笔舔

古代文人用来舔拭毛笔的用具。古人在书写绘画时，有时笔头会有不顺，或有含墨过多的情况，在下笔之前可在笔舔上进行调试，为下笔行文描色作准备。笔舔有瓷、玉、琉璃、水晶等材质。

Writing Brush Tester

Before either writing or painting, ancient people used a tester to try the brush tip for the amount of ink it contained, to make sure the hairs were neat and orderly, and the ink amount was right, neither too much nor too little. This was a tool to avoid inconsistency in shades. Common materials for the testers included porcelain, jade, colored glaze or crystal.

• 白釉荷叶式笔舔（五代）
White Glazed Lotus Leaf Writing Brush Tester (Five Dynasties, 907-960)

• 仿官窑笔舔（清）
Tester, Imitation of Product From an Official Kiln (Qing Dynasty, 1616-1911)

• 象牙笔掭（清）
Ivory Writing Brush Tester (Qing Dynasty, 1616-1911)

笔床

用来卧放毛笔的用具，在性能上相当于笔盒。笔床有鎏金、翡翠、瓷、紫檀、乌木等材质，现在能见到的笔床多为瓷和竹木制品。

Writing Brush Bed

The tool that writing brushes "sleep" upon, is similar in function to a brush box. Common materials for the bed included porcelain, emerald, rosewood and ebony. Some were gold plated. Most of the beds we can see today are either of porcelain, bamboo or wood.

• 青花描金粉彩山水人物纹笔床（清）
Blue-and-white, Gold-traced, Patterned Writing Brush Bed with Landscape and Human Figure (Qing Dynasty, 1616-1911)

墨床

古人在研磨墨停顿下来时，用来放墨锭的文房用具。研墨停顿时，墨锭一头沾有墨汁，若随意放很容易弄脏别处，墨床就用来临时搁置墨锭。墨床的体积不大，多以小巧秀美取胜。常见的墨床形状包括几形、多宝槅形、盒形等。

Ink Bed

For temporary placement of an ink stick between grindings. One end of the stick had ink. To avoid a mess on the desk this ink stick bed came into being. Usually, the bed was small, but very exquisite and attractive in looks. Common appearances included geometric forms, a shelf in ancient style or simply a box.

- 白玉俎式墨床（清）
White Jade Ink Stick Bed (Qing Dynasty, 1616-1911)

- 水晶墨床（清）
Crystal Ink Stick Bed (Qing Dynasty, 1616-1911)

- 黄玛瑙竹节式墨床（清）
Yellow Agate Bamboo-joint Ink Stick Bed (Qing Dynasty, 1616-1911)

- 白玉墨床（清）
White Jade Ink Stick Bed (Qing Dynasty, 1616-1911)

书镇

又名"镇纸",是压纸张的用具,其功能一是防止纸被风吹走,二是可以把纸抻平,便于写字作画。有的镇纸做成尺子的形状,所以又名"镇尺"。镇纸集实用性与观赏性于一体,造型变化多样,但不论造型如何,都有底部平整、重心低、有一定的重量、表面光洁四个基本特点。

Book Weight

Also called paper weight, something to keep paper from being blown away by wind. It had another function: keep paper smooth for writing and painting. Some paperweights were made like rulers. No matter the appearances, they were both practical in use and beautiful to look at. They had a very at and smooth bottom, low center of gravity, weighty and smooth surface.

- 铜狮镇纸(清)

Copper Lion Paperweight (Qing Dynasty, 1616-1911)

- 青玉天鹅形镇纸(清)

Gray Jade Swan Paperweight (Qing Dynasty, 1616-1911)

- 青玉"三阳开泰"镇纸(清)

Gray Jade Paperweight with Auspicious Symbols (Qing Dynasty, 1616-1911)

- 翡翠圆形镇纸(清)

Emerald Round Paperweight (Qing Dynasty, 1616-1911)

附录:其他文房用具

Appendix: Other Tools in a Traditional Chinese Study

• 紫檀木嵌竹刻书镇（现代）
Rosewood Inlaid with Bamboo Inscription Paperweight (Modern Times)

• 竹雕镇纸（现代）
Inscribed Bamboo Paperweight (Modern Times)

臂搁

用来搁手臂的一种文房用具，在宋代就已出现。古人写毛笔字的顺序是从右往左，从上往下，在换行的时候手腕正好在刚写好的字上，容易把字蹭花，把衣服弄脏，臂搁的制作与使用解决了这一问题。臂搁上常雕饰花纹，有很高的观赏价值。

Arm Pillow

It was first seen during the Song Dynasty. Ancient people wrote from right to left and from top to bottom. When they were changing a line, their wrist was just above the characters freshly written, therefore it's common to get characters smeared and sleeves stained. Arm pillows solved this problem. Being beautifully carved, these pillows were works of art.

• 青玉竹节臂搁（明）
Gray Jade Bamboo-joint Arm Pillow (Ming Dynasty, 1368-1644)

• 翡翠臂搁（清）
Emerald Arm Pillow (Qing Dynasty, 1616-1911)

- 留青竹刻荷塘纹臂搁（清）
Arm Pillow Inscribed with Bamboo (Qing Dynasty, 1616-1911)

- 平刻象牙婴戏图臂搁（现代）
Ivory Arm Pillow Inscribed with Children (Modern Times)

- 留青花鸟纹竹雕臂搁（清）
Arm Pillow with Flower, Bird and Bamboo (Qing Dynasty, 1616-1911)

- 象牙雕臂搁（现代）
Ivory Inscribed Arm Pillow (Modern Times)

附录：其他文房用具
Appendix: Other Tools in a Traditional Chinese Study

砚滴

又称"水注",是向砚里注水的工具,在西晋已较为流行,宋元时期盛行。砚滴一般做成青蛙、乌龟、瑞兽的形状,摆设在书桌上,也极具观赏价值。尽管砚滴的外形多种多样,但有三点结构是共同的:一是腹内中空,可以盛水;二是在较高的位置上有一细孔,倾倒时,可以滴出水来;三是背上有一个圆孔和腹相通,圆孔上有一段高起的管状器,可以注入水,用水时,用一个手指按住,把砚滴移到砚台上时,不会有水洒出,只要略松开手指,便有水滴到砚台上。

Inkstone Water Filler

A tool that fills water into an inkstone emerged during the Western Jin Dynasty but got popular in the later Song and Yuan dynasties. It was often shaped after a frog, a turtle or some legendary animal, something to be placed on a desk. Apart from its practical use it was pleasant to look at. They shared three common features: hollow inside to keep water, having a small hole on the upper part for water to out ow, and having another hole on top attached to a tube for filling. Keep a finger on this hole before the filler is moved to the inkstone and remove the finger so water drips onto the inkstone.

- 越窑兔形砚滴(三国)
Hare Filler from *Yue* Kiln (Three-Kingdom Period, 220-280)

- 青瓷兔形水注(晋)
Celadon Hare Filler (Jin Dynasty, 265-420)

- 玉兽形砚滴（宋）
Jade Filler in an Animal Shape (Song Dynasty, 960-1279)

- 青白釉凤首流水注（宋）
Glazed Pale Green Filler with a Phoenix Head (Song Dynasty, 960-1279)

- 青玉卧凤砚滴（明）
Pale Green Jade Phoenix Filler (Ming Dynasty, 1368-1644)

- 龙泉窑舟形砚滴（元）
Boat Filler from *Longquan* Kiln (Yuan Dynasty, 1206-1368)

• 宣德款龟形铜砚滴（明）
Copper Turtle Filler in Xuande Style (Ming Dynasty, 1368-1644)

• 铜蟾形砚滴（明）
Copper Toad Filler (Ming Dynasty, 1368-1644)

水盂

又称"水丞"，小型盛水器皿，磨墨时就用小匙从中舀出水来。水盂体形小巧，做工精致，一般配有铜或珊瑚制成的匙。水盂的样式很多，有方形、圆形、海棠形、如意形、桃形、荷叶形、葫芦形、荷叶莲蓬型、鹅形、鸭形、蟾形、海螺形等，口有圆口、葵口、菱口、花口等。

Water Jar

Use a small spoon to ladle water out of this jar for grinding ink. Usually the jar was small but very exquisitely made, often having a copper or coral spoon on one side. They had different shapes, square or round or fashioned after auspicious plants, animals or birds. Their openings varied a lot in shape and size.

• 青釉蛙形水盂（西晋）
Pale Green Glazed Frog Jar (Western Jin Dynasty, 265-316)

• 水晶桃式水盂（明）
Crystal Peach Jar (Ming Dynasty, 1368-1644)

• 天蓝釉小水盂（清）
Azure-blue Glazed Small Jar (Qing Dynasty, 1616-1911)

• 玛瑙荷叶水丞（清）
Agate Lotus Leaf Jar (Qing Dynasty, 1616-1911)

• 铜童戏水盂（清）
Copper Jar of Children Playing with Water (Qing Dynasty, 1616-1911)

- 宜兴窑双螭福寿水丞（清）
  Jar of Yixing Kiln, with Legendary Loongs Standing for Happiness and Longevity (Qing Dynasty, 1616-1911)

- 青玉秋蝉桐叶水丞（清）
  Pale Jade Cicada and Tung-leaf Jar (Qing Dynasty, 1616-1911)

- 清代紫晶玉兰花水丞（清）
  Amethyst Magnolia Flower Jar (Qing Dynasty, 1616-1911)